First Edition

W9-BIE-403

triumphlearning™
Common Core Coach
Mathematics 7

Dr. Jerry Kaplan
Senior Mathematics Consultant

Common Core Coach, Mathematics, First Edition, Grade 7   T118NA   ISBN-13: 978-1-61997-440-1
Contributing Writers: Russell Kahn, Colleen O'Donnell   **Cover Design:** Q2A/Bill Smith   **Cover Illustration:** Elizabeth Rosen

Contents

🔧 Problem Solving   ⚡ Fluency Lesson   🧩 Performance Task

Common Core
State Standards

Grade 6

Grade 7

Grade 8

Grade 6 RP
Understand ratio concepts and use ratio reasoning to solve problems.

Grade 6 NS
Apply and extend previous understandings of multiplication and division to divide fractions by fractions.

Apply and extend previous understandings of numbers to the system of rational numbers.

Grade 6 EE
Reason about and solve one-variable equations and inequalities.

Represent and analyze quantitative relationships between dependent and independent variables.

Grade 7 RP
Analyze proportional relationships and use them to solve real-world and mathematical problems.

Grade 8 EE
Understand the connections between proportional relationships, lines, and linear equations.

Grade 8 F
Define, evaluate, and compare functions.

Use functions to model relationships between quantities.

Grade 8 G
Understand congruence and similarity using physical models, transparencies, or geometry software.

Grade 8 SP
Investigate patterns of association in bivariate data.

Domain 1
Ratios and Proportional Relationships

Computing Unit Rate

A **ratio** is a comparison of two quantities. A **rate** is a type of ratio that compares two quantities that have different units of measure. For example, $30 for 5 pounds is a rate that compares dollars to pounds. If a rate is a **unit rate**, the second quantity in the comparison is 1 unit. For example, $6 per pound is a unit rate because it compares $6 to 1 pound.

If a rate involves comparing two fractions, you can use a **complex fraction** to represent the rate. A complex fraction is a fraction in which the numerator and/or the denominator is a fraction or a mixed number.

EXAMPLE A Evan walks $\frac{5}{8}$ mile every $\frac{1}{4}$ hour. Express his speed as a unit rate in miles per hour.

1

Write the rate as a complex fraction.

$$\frac{\frac{5}{8}\,\text{mi}}{\frac{1}{4}\,\text{h}} = \frac{\frac{5}{8}}{\frac{1}{4}}$$

The denominator is $\frac{1}{4}$, but in a unit rate, the denominator will be 1.

2

Rewrite the complex fraction so that it has a denominator of 1.

Since the denominator is $\frac{1}{4}$, you can multiply it times 4 to get a denominator of 1.

$$\frac{1}{4} \times 4 = \frac{1}{4} \times \frac{4}{1} = 1$$

Multiply both the numerator and the denominator times 4.

$$\frac{\frac{5}{8}}{\frac{1}{4}} \times \frac{4}{4} = \frac{\frac{5}{8} \times \frac{4}{1}}{\frac{1}{4} \times \frac{4}{1}} = \frac{\frac{20}{8}}{1}$$

The result is a denominator of 1. So, the ratio now shows a unit rate.

$$\frac{\frac{20}{8}\,\text{mi}}{1\,\text{h}} = \frac{\frac{5}{2}\,\text{mi}}{1\,\text{h}} = 2\frac{1}{2} \text{ miles per hour}$$

▶ Evan's rate of speed is $2\frac{1}{2}$ miles per hour.

TRY

Ariella jogs $3\frac{1}{8}$ miles in $\frac{5}{8}$ hour. Express her speed as a unit rate in miles per hour.

EXAMPLE B A recipe calls for $1\frac{1}{2}$ cups of flour for every $\frac{3}{4}$ cup of sugar used. How many cups of flour are needed for each cup of sugar used?

1

Write the ratio as a complex fraction.

Convert $1\frac{1}{2}$ to an improper fraction: $1\frac{1}{2} = \frac{1 \times 2 + 1}{2} = \frac{3}{2}$ The ratio is: $\dfrac{\frac{3}{2} \text{ c flour}}{\frac{3}{4} \text{ c sugar}} = \dfrac{\frac{3}{2}}{\frac{3}{4}}$.

2

Use a fraction model.

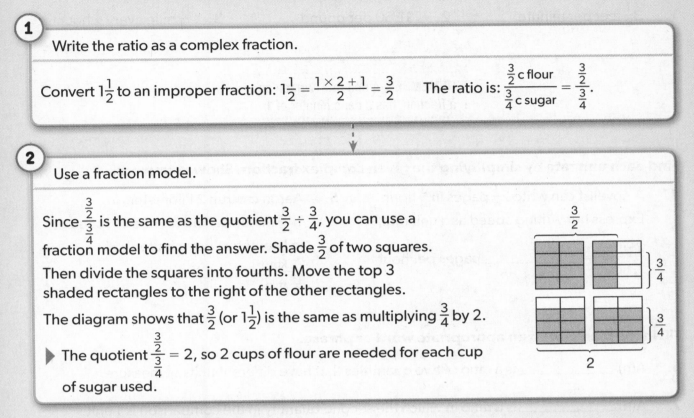

Since $\dfrac{\frac{3}{2}}{\frac{3}{4}}$ is the same as the quotient $\frac{3}{2} \div \frac{3}{4}$, you can use a fraction model to find the answer. Shade $\frac{3}{2}$ of two squares.

Then divide the squares into fourths. Move the top 3 shaded rectangles to the right of the other rectangles.

The diagram shows that $\frac{3}{2}$ (or $1\frac{1}{2}$) is the same as multiplying $\frac{3}{4}$ by 2.

▶ The quotient $\dfrac{\frac{3}{2}}{\frac{3}{4}} = 2$, so 2 cups of flour are needed for each cup of sugar used.

EXAMPLE C A motorized scooter can travel $5\frac{3}{4}$ miles on $\frac{1}{5}$ gallon of gasoline. How many miles per gallon does the scooter get?

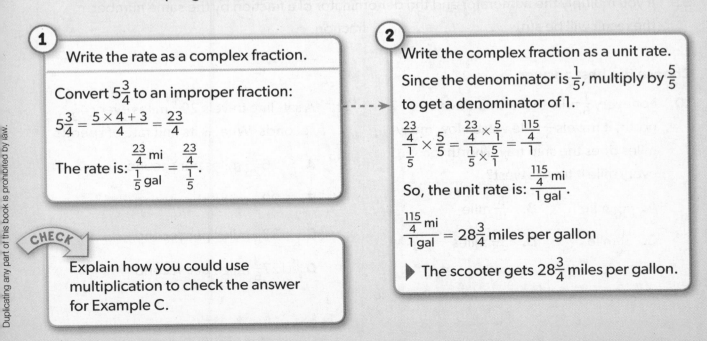

1

Write the rate as a complex fraction.

Convert $5\frac{3}{4}$ to an improper fraction:

$5\frac{3}{4} = \frac{5 \times 4 + 3}{4} = \frac{23}{4}$

The rate is: $\dfrac{\frac{23}{4} \text{ mi}}{\frac{1}{5} \text{ gal}} = \dfrac{\frac{23}{4}}{\frac{1}{5}}$.

CHECK

Explain how you could use multiplication to check the answer for Example C.

2

Write the complex fraction as a unit rate.

Since the denominator is $\frac{1}{5}$, multiply by $\frac{5}{5}$ to get a denominator of 1.

$\dfrac{\frac{23}{4}}{\frac{1}{5}} \times \frac{5}{5} = \dfrac{\frac{23}{4} \times \frac{5}{1}}{\frac{1}{5} \times \frac{5}{1}} = \dfrac{\frac{115}{4}}{1}$

So, the unit rate is: $\dfrac{\frac{115}{4} \text{ mi}}{1 \text{ gal}}$.

$\dfrac{\frac{115}{4} \text{ mi}}{1 \text{ gal}} = 28\frac{3}{4}$ miles per gallon

▶ The scooter gets $28\frac{3}{4}$ miles per gallon.

Practice

Classify each rate. Write *unit rate* or *not a unit rate*.

1. $3\frac{1}{2}$ feet per minute

2. $1.60 per pound

3. $\frac{1}{4}$ mile every $\frac{1}{6}$ hour

_____   _____   _____

> **REMEMBER** A unit rate, written as a fraction, has a denominator of 1.

Find each unit rate by simplifying the given complex fraction. Show your work.

4. A novelist can write $2\frac{1}{4}$ pages in $\frac{3}{4}$ hour. Express her writing speed as a unit rate.

$\dfrac{\frac{9}{4}\ \text{pages}}{\frac{3}{4}\ \text{hour}} = $ _____ pages per hour

5. Aaron can run 2 kilometers in $14\frac{1}{2}$ minutes. Find his rate of speed in kilometers per minute.

$\dfrac{2\ \text{km}}{\frac{29}{2}\ \text{min}} = $ _____

Fill in the blanks with an appropriate word or phrase.

6. A(n) _____ is a ratio of two quantities that have different units of measure.

7. A(n) _____ is a ratio in which the second quantity in the comparison is 1 unit.

8. A(n) _____ fraction has a fraction in the numerator, the denominator, or both.

9. If you multiply the numerator and the denominator of a fraction by the same number, the result will be a(n) _____ fraction.

Choose the best answer.

10. For every $\frac{1}{6}$ mile that a ship travels north, it travels $\frac{3}{5}$ mile west. How many miles does the ship travel north for every mile it travels west?

    A. $\frac{1}{10}$ mile
    B. $\frac{5}{18}$ mile
    C. $\frac{1}{3}$ mile
    D. $3\frac{3}{5}$ miles

11. A satellite travels $29\frac{1}{2}$ miles every $4\frac{1}{3}$ seconds. What is its unit rate of speed?

    A. $6\frac{21}{26}$ miles per second
    B. $29\frac{1}{2}$ miles per second
    C. $33\frac{5}{6}$ miles per second
    D. $127\frac{5}{6}$ miles per second

Find each unit rate. Show your work.

12. Renting an office costs $486 per month. The office has an area of $202\frac{1}{2}$ square feet. What is the monthly cost per square foot to rent the office?

_____

13. A recipe calls for using $\frac{3}{4}$ cup of brown sugar for each $\frac{2}{3}$ cup of white sugar. How many cups of brown sugar are used per cup of white sugar?

_____

14. Lauren bikes $1\frac{1}{3}$ miles in $\frac{1}{10}$ hour. What is her rate of speed in miles per hour?

_____

15. Oliver reads $28\frac{1}{2}$ pages of a book in $1\frac{1}{6}$ hours. Express his reading speed in pages per hour.

_____

Solve.

16. **SHOW** On mountainous terrain, a semi-truck travels $2\frac{2}{3}$ miles on $\frac{1}{2}$ gallon of fuel. How many miles can the truck travel per gallon of fuel? Use drawings or equations to show your work.

17. **EXPLAIN** A car travels $\frac{2}{5}$ mile in $\frac{1}{2}$ minute. What is the car's speed in miles per **hour**? Explain how you determined your answer.

_____

_____

_____

Identifying Proportional Relationships

UNDERSTAND A **proportion** states that two ratios are equivalent. In a proportional relationship, when one quantity increases, the other quantity also increases. The ratio of the two quantities remains constant. This constant ratio is called the **constant of proportionality**, k.

You can use tables, graphs, or equations to determine if relationships are directly proportional.

- Test pairs of values in a table to see if they are equivalent ratios.

- Graph pairs of values to see if they form a straight line that passes through the **origin**.

- Test pairs of values to see if they are related by the equation $y = kx$, where k is the constant of proportionality.

If the above are true, the quantities are in a directly proportional relationship.

Show that the quantities in the table below are in a directly proportional relationship. Identify the constant of proportionality, which is also Tina's hourly wage.

Tina's Earnings

Hours Worked (x)	1	2	3	4	5	6
Total Earnings in $ (y)	12	24	36	48	60	72

1

Write pairs of values as ratios. Simplify them.

$\frac{1}{12}$ is in simplest form. $\frac{2}{24} = \frac{2 \div 2}{24 \div 2} = \frac{1}{12}$ $\frac{3}{36} = \frac{3 \div 3}{36 \div 3} = \frac{1}{12}$

$\frac{4}{48} = \frac{4 \div 4}{48 \div 4} = \frac{1}{12}$ $\frac{5}{60} = \frac{5 \div 5}{60 \div 5} = \frac{1}{12}$ $\frac{6}{72} = \frac{6 \div 6}{72 \div 6} = \frac{1}{12}$

The quantities are in a proportional relationship because each simplifies to $\frac{1}{12}$.

You can write this proportion: $\frac{1}{12} = \frac{2}{24} = \frac{3}{36} = \frac{4}{48} = \frac{5}{60} = \frac{6}{72}$.

2

Determine the constant of proportionality, which is also Tina's hourly wage.

Her wage will be in dollars per hour. So, write and simplify ratios comparing $\frac{dollars}{hours}$.

Each ratio in the table is equivalent, so you can use any ratio to determine the constant:

$\frac{\$12}{1\,h} = \$12$ per hour   or $\frac{\$24}{2\,h} = \frac{\$12}{1\,h} = \$12$ per hour

Since the denominator of each ratio is 1 hour, the constant of proportionality is also a unit rate.

▶ The quantities in the table are equivalent ratios, so this shows a proportional relationship. The constant of proportionality is 12, so Tina's hourly wage is $12 per hour.

⊶ Connect

Use the table of data on the preceding page to create a graph. Explain how the graph shows that the quantities are in a proportional relationship. Then use the graph to identify the constant of proportionality.

1

Plot and label the ordered pairs from the table on a coordinate grid.

Connect the points.

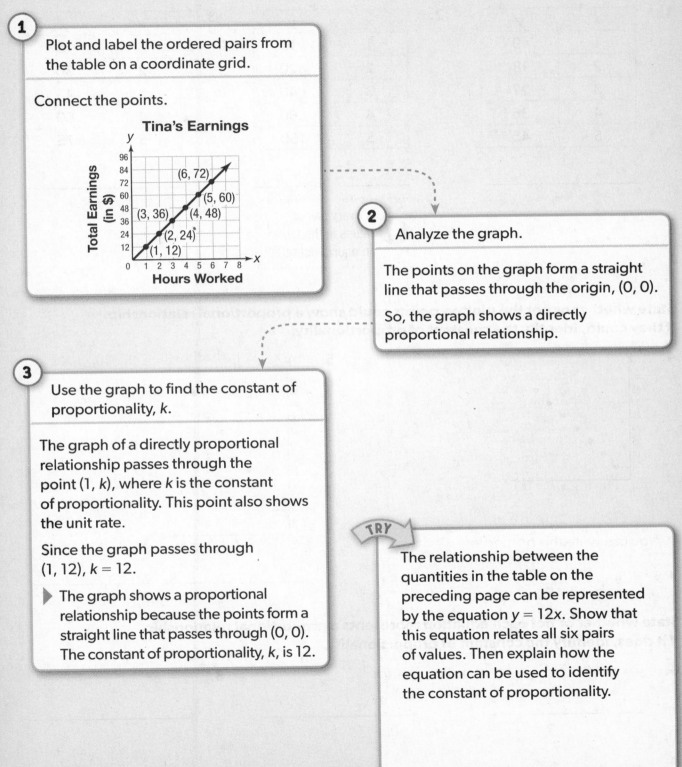

Tina's Earnings

(6, 72)
(5, 60)
(3, 36)   (4, 48)
(2, 24)
(1, 12)

Total Earnings (in $)

Hours Worked

2

Analyze the graph.

The points on the graph form a straight line that passes through the origin, (0, 0).

So, the graph shows a directly proportional relationship.

3

Use the graph to find the constant of proportionality, k.

The graph of a directly proportional relationship passes through the point $(1, k)$, where k is the constant of proportionality. This point also shows the unit rate.

Since the graph passes through $(1, 12)$, $k = 12$.

▶ The graph shows a proportional relationship because the points form a straight line that passes through $(0, 0)$. The constant of proportionality, k, is 12.

TRY

The relationship between the quantities in the table on the preceding page can be represented by the equation $y = 12x$. Show that this equation relates all six pairs of values. Then explain how the equation can be used to identify the constant of proportionality.

Practice

State whether or not each table shows a proportional relationship. If it does, identify the constant of proportionality.

1.

x	y
1	9
2	18
3	27
4	36
5	45

_____

2.

x	y
1	10
2	20
3	40
4	80
5	160

_____

3.

x	y
1	15
2	30
3	45
4	60
5	75

_____

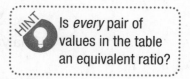

HINT Is *every* pair of values in the table an equivalent ratio?

State whether or not the plotted points could show a proportional relationship. If they could, identify the constant of proportionality.

4.

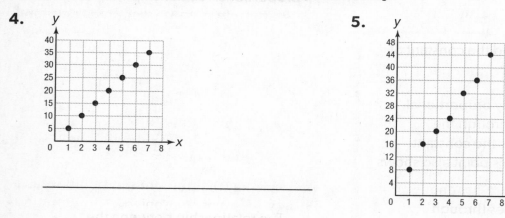

_____

5.

_____

State whether or not each equation represents a proportional relationship. If it does, identify the constant of proportionality.

6. $y = x - 2$

_____

7. $y = 7x$

_____

8. $y = \frac{1}{5}x$

_____

State whether or not each phrase represents a proportional relationship. Explain how you determined your answer, and if proportional, identify the constant of proportionality.

9. The value of *y* is equal to three times the value of *x*.

_____

10. The value of *y* is equal to the sum of *x* and nine.

_____

Each mapping diagram shows a relationship between *x*-values and *y*-values. State whether or not each diagram represents a proportional relationship. Explain how you determined your answer, and if proportional, identify the constant of proportionality.

11.

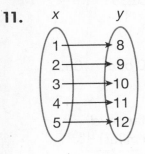

_____

12.

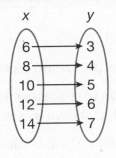

_____

Solve.

13. **WRITE MATH** Zivia is given the ordered pair (4, 16) from a table. She decides that the quantities in the table form a proportional relationship with a constant of proportionality of 4. Write whether Zivia has enough information to draw her conclusion.

_____

_____

_____

14. **EXPLAIN** The formula for the circumference of a circle is $C = \pi d$, where *C* is the circumference and *d* is the diameter of the circle. Is this an example of a proportional relationship? If so, identify the constant of proportionality. Explain your reasoning.

_____

_____

_____

Representing Proportional Relationships

UNDERSTAND You can represent a directly proportional relationship by an equation in the form of $y = kx$, where k is the constant of proportionality or unit rate.

You can use an equation to represent a verbal description of a directly proportional relationship.

For a babysitting job, the total charge is equal to the number of hours worked times $10,

c $=$ h $\times$ 10

▶ The verbal description can be represented by the equation $c = h \times 10$ or $c = 10h$.

You can use an equation to represent a directly proportional relationship shown in a table.

As the t-values increase by 1, the d-values increase by 60. So, the distance, d, is equal to the time, t, times 60.

Time, t (in hours)	Distance, d (in miles)
1	60
2	120
3	180
4	240

+1 / +60
+1 / +60
+1 / +60

▶ The situation can be represented by the equation $d = t \times 60$ or $d = 60t$.

You can use an equation to represent a directly proportional relationship shown in a graph.

The graph shows that for each additional 1 pound of peppers purchased, the total cost increases by $4. So, the total cost, c, is equal to the number of pounds, p, times 4.

▶ The graph can be represented by the equation $c = p \times 4$ or $c = 4p$.

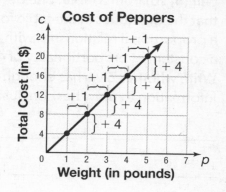

Cost of Peppers

⊸Connect

Another way to determine the constant of proportionality is to examine a graph that shows a directly proportional relationship. The point $(1, k)$ shows the constant of proportionality, which is also the unit rate. If you are looking for a unit rate, r, you can think of this point as $(1, r)$.

This graph shows the rate at which water is flowing from a faucet into a bathtub. What does the point $(4, 8)$ on the graph represent? Which point represents the unit rate, and what is the unit rate?

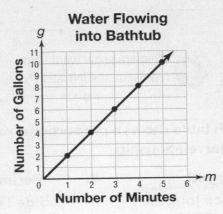

1 Use the graph to examine the proportional relationship.

What does the point $(4, 8)$ represent?

The horizontal axis shows the number of minutes that have passed.

The vertical axis shows the number of gallons of water in the tub after that many minutes.

So, $(4, 8)$ shows that after 4 minutes, there will be 8 gallons of water in the tub.

2 Find the unit rate.

The graph of a proportional relationship passes through the points $(0, 0)$ and $(1, r)$, where r represents the unit rate.

The graph passes through $(0, 0)$ and $(1, 2)$.

So, the unit rate is 2 gallons per minute.

▶ The point $(4, 8)$ represents the number of gallons of water in the tub, 8, after 4 minutes have passed. The unit rate is represented by the point $(1, 2)$. That point shows that water is flowing into the tub at a rate of 2 gallons per minute.

TRY

What does the point $\left(\frac{1}{2}, 1\right)$ represent on the graph?

Practice

Write an equation to represent each proportional relationship described below.

1. The height of a building, h, is equal to the number of floors, f, times 11 feet.

   _____

2. The download time, t, is equal to the product of the number of gigabytes, g, and 3 minutes.

   _____

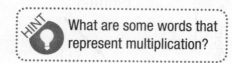

HINT What are some words that represent multiplication?

Determine whether or not each table shows a proportional relationship. If it does, write an equation for the proportional relationship.

3. **Total Distance Jogged**

Time (in minutes), t	Distance Jogged (in meters), d
1	100
2	220
3	330
4	450

_____

4. **Perimeter of Regular Hexagon**

Side Length, s (in units)	Perimeter, P (in units)
1	6
2	12
3	18
4	24

HINT Do the values in each column increase by the same amounts?

Use the graph on the right for questions 5–7.

5. Explain how you know that this graph shows a proportional relationship.

   _____

6. What does the point (5, 350) represent on the graph?

   _____

7. Which point on the graph shows the unit rate for this situation, and what is the unit rate?

   _____

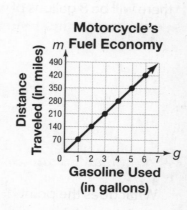

Motorcycle's Fuel Economy

Distance Traveled (in miles)

Gasoline Used (in gallons)

Determine whether or not the equation shows a proportional relationship. If it does, identify the unit rate (constant of proportionality).

8. $y = 25x$

_____

9. $a = 5x + 5$

_____

10. $m = 105.25n$

_____

Choose the best answer.

11. Which equation best represents the relationship in the table?

x	y
$\frac{1}{2}$	$2\frac{1}{2}$
1	5
$1\frac{1}{2}$	$7\frac{1}{2}$
2	10
$2\frac{1}{2}$	$12\frac{1}{2}$
3	15

A. $y = x + \frac{5}{2}$

B. $y = 5x + 5$

C. $y = 5x$

D. $y = \frac{5}{2}x$

12. The point (1.5, 0.15) is on the graph below. What does that point represent?

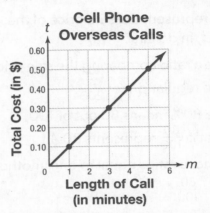

Cell Phone Overseas Calls

A. A call that lasts 0.15 minute will cost $1.50.

B. A call that lasts 1.5 minutes will cost $0.15.

C. The unit rate is $0.15 per minute.

D. The unit rate is $1.50 per minute.

Solve.

13. **EXPLAIN** The graph of a proportional relationship passes through the points (2, 22) and (4, 44). Explain how you know the *r*-value for the point (1, *r*).

_____

_____

_____

14. **WRITE MATH** Write a real-life problem situation that could be represented by the equation $y = 65x$. State what *x*, *y*, and 65 represent in your problem and explain how you know that the problem represents a proportional relationship.

_____

_____

_____

LESSON 4 — Word Problems with Ratio and Percent

EXAMPLE A The regular price of a jacket is $200. Today the jacket is on sale. It costs 80% of its regular price. The sales tax is 8%. If Stefan buys the jacket today, how much will he pay in total once tax is added?

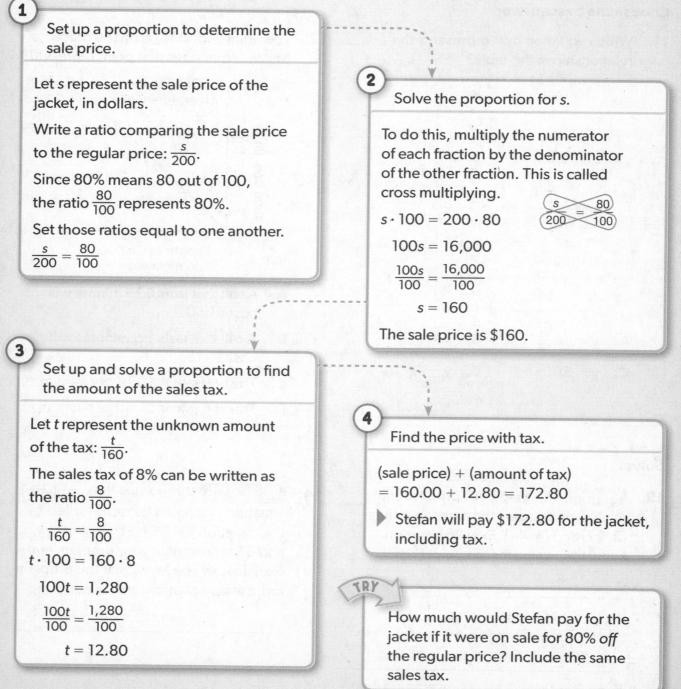

1

Set up a proportion to determine the sale price.

Let s represent the sale price of the jacket, in dollars.

Write a ratio comparing the sale price to the regular price: $\frac{s}{200}$.

Since 80% means 80 out of 100, the ratio $\frac{80}{100}$ represents 80%.

Set those ratios equal to one another.

$\frac{s}{200} = \frac{80}{100}$

2

Solve the proportion for s.

To do this, multiply the numerator of each fraction by the denominator of the other fraction. This is called cross multiplying.

$s \cdot 100 = 200 \cdot 80$

$\frac{s}{200} = \frac{80}{100}$

$100s = 16{,}000$

$\frac{100s}{100} = \frac{16{,}000}{100}$

$s = 160$

The sale price is $160.

3

Set up and solve a proportion to find the amount of the sales tax.

Let t represent the unknown amount of the tax: $\frac{t}{160}$.

The sales tax of 8% can be written as the ratio $\frac{8}{100}$.

$\frac{t}{160} = \frac{8}{100}$

$t \cdot 100 = 160 \cdot 8$

$100t = 1{,}280$

$\frac{100t}{100} = \frac{1{,}280}{100}$

$t = 12.80$

4

Find the price with tax.

(sale price) + (amount of tax)
= 160.00 + 12.80 = 172.80

▶ Stefan will pay $172.80 for the jacket, including tax.

TRY

How much would Stefan pay for the jacket if it were on sale for 80% *off* the regular price? Include the same sales tax.

EXAMPLE B The population of a city in the year 2000 was 4,400. In 2010, the population was 5,060. Find the percent increase in the population from 2000 to 2010. Assuming the population continues to grow at the same rate, predict what the population will be in 2020.

1

Find the amount of the increase in population.

amount of = (population in 2010) −
increase   (population in 2000)

amount of increase = 5,060 − 4,400
                   = 660

2

Find the percent increase from 2000 to 2010.

Let p represent the percent increase. So, one ratio is $\frac{p}{100}$.

The other ratio should compare the amount of the increase to the original population: $\frac{660}{4400}$.

$$\frac{p}{100} = \frac{660}{4400}$$

$$4400p = 66,000$$

$$p = 15$$

▶ The percent increase is 15%.

3

Set up a proportion to predict the population in 2020.

Assume the population will increase by about 15%.

If so, the new population, n, in 2020 will be 100% + 15%, or 115%, of the 2010 population.

$$\frac{115}{100} = \frac{n}{5060}$$

4

Solve the proportion for n.

$$\frac{115}{100} = \frac{n}{5060}$$

$$581,900 = 100n$$

$$5,819 = n$$

▶ A good prediction of what the city's population will be in 2020 is 5,819.

TRY

Extend the problem to predict the population of the city in 2030. Explain why you have to round the answer to a whole number.

EXAMPLE C A salesperson earns a 5% commission on all jewelry sold. This week, she earns a $400 commission. She wants to earn a $500 commission next week. What increase in total sales would she need in order to earn a $500 commission next week?

1

Set up a proportion to find her total sales, in dollars, for this week.

Her commission is a fraction of t, her total sales for this week. So, one ratio is $\frac{400}{t}$.

Her commission is 5%, so use $\frac{5}{100}$ as the other ratio.

$$\frac{400}{t} = \frac{5}{100}$$

2

Solve the proportion for t.

$$\frac{400}{t} = \frac{5}{100}$$

$$40{,}000 = 5t$$

$$8{,}000 = t$$

The salesperson sold $8,000 worth of jewelry this week.

3

Set up a proportion to find the amount of jewelry she would need to sell to make $500 next week.

Let n represent her total sales for next week if she earns a $500 commission.

$$\frac{500}{n} = \frac{5}{100}$$

$$50{,}000 = 5n$$

$$10{,}000 = n$$

4

Solve the problem.

The question asked, "What increase in total sales" the salesperson would need. Subtract.

(sales for a $500 commission) − (sales for a $400 commission)
= 10,000 − 8,000 = 2,000

▶ The salesperson needs to increase her total sales by $2,000 in order to earn the increased commission.

CHECK

Find the commission for selling $2,000 worth of jewelry. Explain how you can use that amount to check your answer.

EXAMPLE D You can use a proportion to find a percent error.

Five lab partner pairs come up with 5 different measurements for the mass of an object. The measurements were 187 g, 206 g, 212 g, 194 g, and 216 g. The actual mass of the object was 200 g. What was the percent error in the average of their measurements?

1

Find the average of the measurements.

$$\text{mean} = \frac{187 + 206 + 212 + 194 + 216}{5}$$

$$= \frac{1{,}015}{5} = 203$$

$|203 - 200| = 3$, so the difference between the actual mass and the average of the measurements is 3 grams.

2

Set up a proportion to find the percent error.

Use p to represent the percent error. So, $\frac{p}{100}$ is one ratio.

The percent error is the absolute value of the difference between an estimate and an actual value, divided by the actual value. So, the other ratio is $\frac{3}{200}$.

$$\frac{p}{100} = \frac{3}{200}$$

3

Solve the proportion for p.

$$\frac{p}{100} = \frac{3}{200}$$

$$200p = 300$$

$$p = 1.5$$

The percent error is 1.5%.

▶ The lab partners' percent error in the average of their measurements was 1.5%.

DISCUSS

If the difference between the average of the measurements and the actual mass of the object were 1 gram, would the percent error be greater than or less than 1.5%? Explain.

Practice

Write a proportion that could be used to solve for the unknown in each of the following situations. Then solve for the unknown.

1. Sam's bill at a restaurant is $12, and he leaves a 20% tip. What is the amount of the tip?

_____

2. A $60 sweater is on sale for 25% off. What is the sale price of the sweater?

_____

Complete the proportions. Use them to solve each problem. Show your work.

3. Anna opens two savings accounts at the beginning of a year. She deposits $5,000 in an account that earns 2% interest each year. She deposits $10,000 in a second account that earns 2.5% interest each year. If she makes no withdrawals or deposits, what will be the sum of the interest she earns from her first account (*a*) and second account (*b*) by the end of the year?

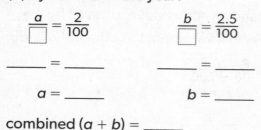

$$\frac{a}{\square} = \frac{2}{100} \qquad \frac{b}{\square} = \frac{2.5}{100}$$

_____ = _____   _____ = _____

a = _____   *b* = _____

combined (*a* + *b*) = _____

4. Mr. Abad earned $30,000 last year. He must pay taxes of 10% on earnings up to $8,500, and he must pay taxes of 15% on the rest of his income. What is the total amount he must pay in taxes for his earnings last year, including the taxes on his first $8,500, *f*, and on the rest of his earnings, *r*?

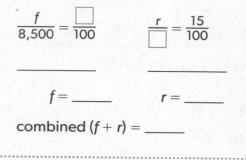

$$\frac{f}{8,500} = \frac{\square}{100} \qquad \frac{r}{\square} = \frac{15}{100}$$

_____   _____

f = _____   *r* = _____

combined (*f* + *r*) = _____

> **HINT** To cross multiply, multiply the numerator of each fraction by the denominator of the other fraction.

Choose the best answer.

5. The adult population of a town in 2000 was 400. The child population of the town in 2000 was 120. Both the adult and child populations increased by the same percent from 2000 to 2010. If the adult population in 2010 was 500, how many children lived in the town?

A. 150   **B.** 145

C. 125   **D.** 30

6. The price of a hard drive decreased from $180 to $144. The price then decreased again by the same percentage as it had during the first decrease. What is the difference between the original price of the hard drive and its new cost?

A. $64.80   **B.** $65.80

C. $108.00   **D.** $115.20

Write and solve proportions to solve each problem. Show your work.

7. At the ABC Electronics Store, a laptop computer was marked down 15% from its original price of $900. A store employee gets an additional 20% discount on the already marked-down price. How much does the employee pay for the laptop computer?

8. A car dealer earns a 4% commission on all cars sold. Last month, he earned $7,200 in commission. He wants to earn $8,000 in commission this month. What increase in total sales from last month's total sales does he need in order to reach his goal for this month?

9. A wholesaler buys pairs of sunglasses for $5.50 each. He then marks up the wholesale cost 80% to create a retail price for his customers. Customers must then pay an additional 7% tax on the retail price. What is the total cost of a pair of sunglasses to the wholesaler's customers, including tax, rounded to the nearest penny?

10. A real-estate agent earns a commission on a house she sells. Her commission is 5% on the first $500,000 of the sale price of the house. She then earns a 6% commission for the amount above $500,000 of the sale price of the house. How much commission did the agent earn if she sold a house for $585,000?

Solve.

11. COMPARE The price for two pairs of jeans is the same, $50. One pair is discounted twice: first for 10% off, then again for 15% off the discounted price. The other pair is discounted once for 25% off. After their respective discounts, are the two pairs of jeans the same price? If not, which is cheaper? Show and explain your work.

12. SHOW A polling company took 5 polls in the week before an election. It showed that a mayoral candidate would get 66%, 56%, 55%, 60%, and 63% of the total votes. That candidate received 64% of the total votes during the actual election. Find the percent error in the average of the company's polling results, to the nearest tenth of a percent. Show your work.

Choose the best answer.

1. A recipe calls for $2\frac{1}{4}$ teaspoons of salt for every $1\frac{1}{8}$ teaspoons of black pepper used. How many teaspoons of salt are needed for each teaspoon of pepper used?

   A. 2 teaspoons

   B. $1\frac{7}{8}$ teaspoons

   C. $1\frac{1}{2}$ teaspoons

   D. $\frac{1}{2}$ teaspoon

2. Aaron designed a robot for a contest. His robot can move $\frac{3}{4}$ meter in $\frac{1}{2}$ second. What is the robot's unit rate of speed?

   A. $\frac{3}{8}$ meter per second

   B. $\frac{2}{3}$ meter per second

   C. $1\frac{1}{2}$ meters per second

   D. $2\frac{1}{2}$ meters per second

Write the constant of proportionality for the pairs of values in each table.

3.

x	1	2	3	4	5	6
y	2.5	5	7.5	10	12.5	15

Constant of proportionality: _____

4.

x	10	20	30	40	50	60
y	1	2	3	4	5	6

Constant of proportionality: _____

Write an equation for each proportional relationship.

5. **Cost of Potato Salad at Deli**

Number of Pounds, p	Total Cost (in $), c
1	3.50
2	7.00
3	10.50
4	14.00
5	17.50

_____

6. **Time to Assemble Swing Sets**

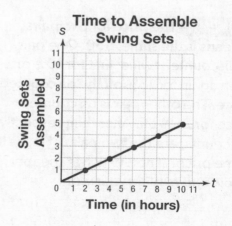

_____

Identify the constant of proportionality for the proportional relationship represented by each equation.

7. $y = 10x$
Constant of
proportionality: _____

8. $y = -x$
Constant of
proportionality: _____

9. $y = 0.27x$
Constant of
proportionality: _____

Choose the best answer.

10. The wolf population of a park was 200 in the year 2000. It increased by 20% from 2000 to 2005. It then increased by 15% from 2005 to 2010. What was the wolf population in the park in 2010?

A. 235

B. 253

C. 270

D. 276

11. The price of a family dinner was $48.00. A sales tax added 5% to the final bill. The family then left a $10.08 tip. If the family included the sales tax when calculating the tip, what percent tip did the family leave?

A. 2%

B. 10%

C. 18%

D. 20%

12. What is the unit rate of speed for this train?

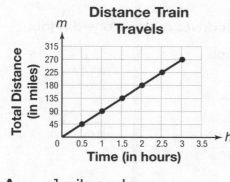

Distance Train Travels

A. 1 mile per hour

B. 45 miles per hour

C. 90 miles per hour

D. 180 miles per hour

13. Which table shows pairs of values that are **not** in a proportional relationship?

A.

x	1	2	3	4
y	14	28	42	56

B.

x	1	2	3	4
y	8	16	32	64

C.

x	1	2	3	4
y	3	6	9	12

D.

x	1	2	3	4
y	$\frac{1}{6}$	$\frac{1}{3}$	$\frac{1}{2}$	$\frac{2}{3}$

For each situation, write a complex fraction. Then compute the unit rate.

14. Andre reads $2\frac{1}{2}$ pages in $\frac{1}{4}$ hour.

complex fraction: _____

unit rate: _____

15. Kelly's car gets $26\frac{1}{4}$ miles per $\frac{5}{8}$ gallon of gas.

complex fraction: _____

unit rate: _____

Solve.

16. **IDENTIFY** The mapping diagram shows that there is a proportional relationship between x-values and y-values.

Identify the constant of proportionality from the diagram. Then write an equation to represent the relationship shown by the diagram. Does your equation also show the constant of proportionality? Explain.

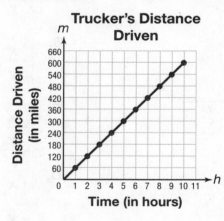

_____

_____

_____

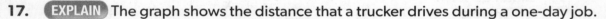

17. **EXPLAIN** The graph shows the distance that a trucker drives during a one-day job.

Trucker's Distance Driven

Distance Driven (in miles) vs. *Time (in hours)*

Does this graph show a proportional relationship? If so, what do the following points represent in this situation: (1, 60) and (2, 120)? Explain your reasoning.

_____

_____

Population Predictions

Materials:
Internet access

Procedure:
Use the information from the U.S. Census Bureau (census.gov) to find the population of your city/town, county/parish, state/district, and country in 2000 and 2010.

a. Complete the following table with the population data.

	City/Town _____	County/Parish _____	State/District _____	Country _____
2000 Population				
2010 Population				
Population Change (2000–2010)				

b. Find the percent change in each of those populations from 2000 to 2010. You may round your answers. Show the proportions you used to find each percent change.

	City/Town _____	County/Parish _____	State/District _____	Country _____
Percent Change (2000–2010)				

c. Use those percent changes to predict what the populations will be in 2020. Round each prediction to the nearest whole number. Show the proportions you used to make each prediction.

	City/Town _____	County/Parish _____	State/District _____	Country _____
2020 Population (Predicted)				

d. Do you expect that your predictions will predict the exact populations in 2020? Explain why or why not.

_____

_____

Grade 8 NS

Know that there are numbers that are not rational, and approximate them by rational numbers.

Grade 6 NS

Apply and extend previous understandings of multiplication and division to divide fractions by fractions.

Compute fluently with multi-digit numbers and find common factors and multiples.

Apply and extend previous understandings of numbers to the system of rational numbers.

Grade 7 NS

Apply and extend previous understandings of operations with fractions to add, subtract, multiply, and divide rational numbers.

Grade 8 EE

Work with radicals and integer exponents.

Analyze and solve linear equations and pairs of simultaneous linear equations.

Grade 8 F

Define, evaluate, and compare functions.

Use functions to model relationships between quantities.

Domain 2
The Number System

5 Adding and Subtracting Rational Numbers

UNDERSTAND Every **rational number** has a location on the number line. Numbers to the left of 0 on the number line are negative. Numbers to the right of 0 are positive. Any numbers n and $-n$ are opposites, or **additive inverses**. The sum of n and $-n$ is 0.

You can use a number line to add or subtract rational numbers. It may help you to think of the sum of $p + q$ as the number located a distance $|q|$ units from p on the number line.

Find the sum: $-3 + 3$

Use a number line.
-3 is negative, so move 3 units to the *left* of 0, as shown by the blue arrow.
To add positive 3 to that number, move 3 units to the *right* as shown by the green arrow.
The green arrow points to 0, which is the sum.

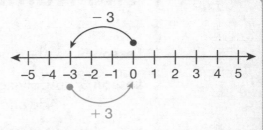

▶ $-3 + 3 = 0$. This makes sense because -3 and 3 are additive inverses.

Matt has a balance of $-\$2.50$ in his bank account. He adds $\$2.50$. Find his new balance.

The blue arrow shows moving from 0 to a point halfway between -3 and -2. That point shows -2.50.
The green arrow models adding 2.50 to that amount. The sum is 0.

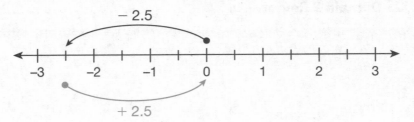

▶ Matt now has a $\$0$ balance in his bank account. -2.50 and 2.50 are additive inverses.

Instead of using a number line to add **integers**, you can look at the signs of the addends:

• If they have the same sign, add their absolute values and give the sum that sign.

• If they have opposite signs, subtract the lesser absolute value from the greater absolute value. Give the sum the sign of the addend with the greater absolute value.

Connect

Use two different methods to find the sum: $-6 + (-4)$

Use a number line and the rule for adding integers with the same sign.

You could use a number line to determine
that $(-6) + (-4) = (-10)$.

Since -6 and -4 have the same sign, you
could also add them like this:

$|-6| + |-4| = 6 + 4 = 10$

Since -6 and -4 are negative,
give the sum a negative sign.

▶ The sum is -10. This shows that $(-) + (-) = (-)$.

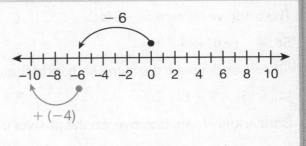

Use two different methods to find the sum: $9 + (-3)$

Use a number line and the rule for adding integers with opposite signs.

You could use a number line to
determine that $(9) + (-3) = 6$.

Since 9 and -3 have opposite signs,
find their difference.

$|9| = 9 \qquad |-3| = 3$

$9 - 3 = 6$

The addend 9 has the greater absolute value, so give the sum a positive sign.

▶ The sum is 6. This shows that sometimes $(+) + (-) = (+)$.

TRY

Choose one method (number line or rules for adding integers). Use it to find the sum:
$4 + (-9)$. Use this example to show that sometimes $(+) + (-) = (-)$.

EXAMPLE A Find the difference: $4 - (-6)$

Rewrite the problem as an addition problem.

The additive inverse of -6 is 6.

So, $4 - (-6) = 4 + 6$.

Since 4 and 6 have the same sign, add their absolute values.

$|4| + |6| = 4 + 6 = 10$

Both addends are positive, so the answer is positive, 10.

▶ $4 - (-6) = 10$

EXAMPLE B Find the difference: $-10 - (-6)$

Rewrite the problem as an addition problem.

The additive inverse of -6 is 6.

So, $-10 - (-6) = -10 + 6$

Since -10 and 6 have opposite signs, subtract the lesser absolute value from the greater absolute value.

$|-10| > |6|$ because $10 > 6$, so:

$|-10| - |6| = 10 - 6 = 4$

Give the answer the sign of the number with the greater absolute value.

Since -10 has the greater absolute value, the answer is -4.

▶ $-10 - (-6) = -4$

MODEL

Draw a model to find the difference: $-3 - 5$.

⚙ Problem Solving

READ

The high temperature in a city one day was 2.6°C. The low temperature was −2.8°C. What was the temperature range in the city that day?

PLAN

The temperature range for the day is equal to the distance between the high temperature and the low temperature.

The distance between two rational numbers on the number line is equal to the absolute value of their difference. Use absolute value to find the answer.

SOLVE

Find the absolute value of the difference: $2.6 - (-2.8)$.

$$|2.6 - (-2.8)| = |2.6 + \underline{\hspace{1cm}}| = |\underline{\hspace{1cm}}| = \underline{\hspace{1cm}}$$

So, the temperature range in the city that day was _____ degrees Celsius.

CHECK

One way to check that the distance between 2.6 and −2.8 is actually the answer you found above is to find the distance between those two numbers on the number line.

Plot points for 2.6 and −2.8 on the number line below. Then count the units between them to check that your answer is correct.

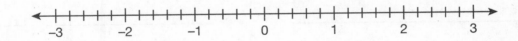

The distance between 2.6 and −2.8 on the number line is _____ units.

Is this the same answer you found above? _____

▶ The range of the temperatures on that day was _____°C.

Practice

Identify the additive inverse, or opposite, of each number.

1. 7

2. −6

3. 9.53

_____   _____   _____

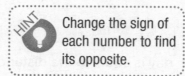

HINT

Change the sign of each number to find its opposite.

Rewrite each subtraction expression as an addition expression.

4. 10 − 5

5. −11.1 − 12.6

6. $\frac{1}{8} - \left(-1\frac{1}{5}\right)$

_____ + _____   _____ + _____   _____ + _____

REMEMBER

The expression $p - q$ is the same as $p + (-q)$.

Use the number line to find each sum or difference. Show your work on the number line.

7. −4 + (−5)

8. −2 + 10

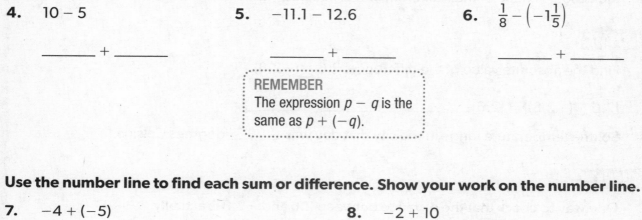

_____   _____

9. 6 − (−4)

10. 5 − 11

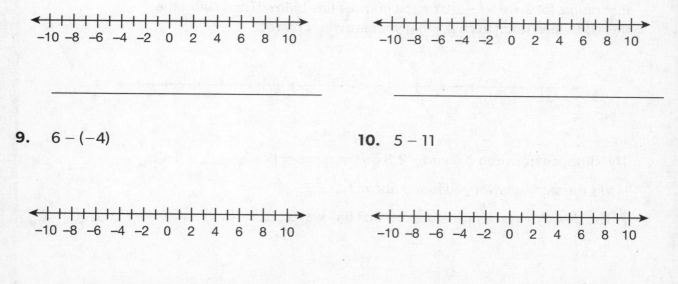

_____   _____

The following thermometers show the range in temperatures in a given day. Find the temperature ranges. Show or explain your work.

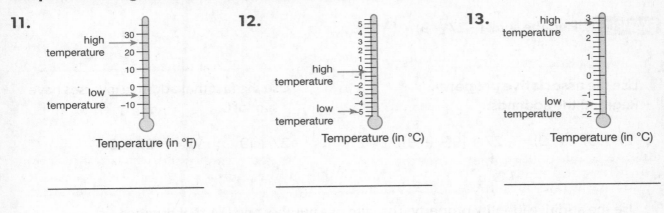

11.

12.

13.

_____

_____

_____

Choose the best answer.

14. A helium atom has 2 electrons, each of which has a −1 charge. Each proton has a +1 charge. Overall, the helium atom has no charge. How many protons must the atom have?

   A. −2   **B.** 0

   C. 2   **D.** 3

15. On January 1, Rose's bank balance was $200. During the month, she wrote checks for $115.25 and $350.00 and made one deposit of $150.50. Which best represents her checking account balance at the end of the month?

   A. −$114.75   **B.** −$114.25

   C. $114.25   **D.** $115.50

Solve.

16. **SHOW** Ira writes that the sum of $a + b$ is a number that is located a distance of $|b|$ units from a on the number line. Choose four values for a and b and show that this is true. Use the four number lines on the right to show your work and support your answer.

   _____

   _____

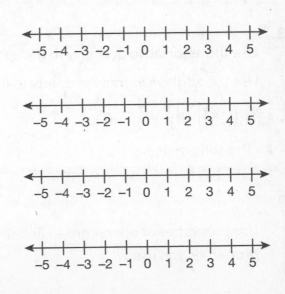

Applying Properties of Operations to Add and Subtract Rational Numbers

EXAMPLE A Find the sum: $(-27 + 9) + (-9)$

1

Use the **associative property**. Regroup the addends.

$(-27 + 9) + (-9) = -27 + [9 + (-9)]$

2

Use the fact that additive inverses have a sum of 0.

$-27 + [9 + (-9)] = -27 + 0$

3

Use the additive identity property. The sum of a number and 0 is that number.

$-27 + 0 = -27$

▶ $(-27 + 9) + (-9) = -27$

EXAMPLE B Simplify the expression: $\frac{3}{4} + \frac{1}{8} - \frac{3}{4} + \frac{7}{8}$

1

Rewrite the subtraction as the addition of the additive inverse.

$\frac{3}{4} + \frac{1}{8} - \frac{3}{4} + \frac{7}{8} = \frac{3}{4} + \frac{1}{8} + \left(-\frac{3}{4}\right) + \frac{7}{8}$

2

Use the **commutative property** to rearrange the addends.

$\frac{3}{4} + \frac{1}{8} + \left(-\frac{3}{4}\right) + \frac{7}{8} = \frac{3}{4} + \left(-\frac{3}{4}\right) + \frac{1}{8} + \frac{7}{8}$

3

Use the associative property to group the like fractions, and add them.

Use the additive identity property to find the final sum.

$\left[\frac{3}{4} + \left(-\frac{3}{4}\right)\right] + \left(\frac{1}{8} + \frac{7}{8}\right) = 0 + 1 = 1$

▶ The solution is 1.

TRY

Use properties of operations to find the sum of $\left(-\frac{7}{10}\right) + \left(\frac{3}{7} + \frac{7}{10}\right)$. Explain which properties you used.

EXAMPLE C Find the sum: $3\frac{1}{6} + \left(-2\frac{3}{4}\right) + 1\frac{2}{6} + 2\frac{3}{4}$

1

Use the commutative property to rearrange the addends and the associative property to group like fractions together.

$3\frac{1}{6} + \left(-2\frac{3}{4}\right) + 1\frac{2}{6} + 2\frac{3}{4}$

$= \left(3\frac{1}{6} + 1\frac{2}{6}\right) + \left(-2\frac{3}{4} + 2\frac{3}{4}\right)$

2

Add the like fractions. Combine the additive inverses.

$\left(3\frac{1}{6} + 1\frac{2}{6}\right) + \left(-2\frac{3}{4} + 2\frac{3}{4}\right) = 4\frac{3}{6} + 0$

Note: You could also write each fraction as a sum, for example: $3\frac{1}{6} = 3 + \frac{1}{6}$, grouping the whole numbers together and the fractions together, if you find it easier to add that way.

3

Use the additive identity property. When you add 0 to a number, the sum is that number.

$4\frac{3}{6} + 0$ becomes $4\frac{3}{6}$, or $4\frac{1}{2}$.

▶ $3\frac{1}{6} + \left(-2\frac{3}{4}\right) + 1\frac{2}{6} + 2\frac{3}{4} = 4\frac{3}{6}$ or $4\frac{1}{2}$

EXAMPLE D Simplify the expression: $4.37 - 1.08 + 2.63 + 1.08$

1

Rewrite the subtraction as addition.

$4.37 - 1.08 + 2.63 + 1.08$
$= 4.37 + (-1.08) + 2.63 + 1.08$

2

Use the commutative and associative properties to rearrange the addends, and group decimals that are easier to add.

$4.37 + (-1.08) + 2.63 + 1.08$
$= (4.37 + 2.63) + (-1.08 + 1.08)$

3

Add the decimals. Combine the additive inverses and apply the additive identity property.

$4.37 + 2.63 + (-1.08 + 1.08) = 7 + 0$
$= 7$

▶ The solution is 7.

DISCUSS

Why is it useful to group certain rational numbers, such as 4.37 and 2.63, together?

Practice

Find each sum.

1. $(7 + 87) + (-7)$

_____

2. $\frac{2}{5} + \frac{1}{3} + \frac{2}{5} + \left(-\frac{1}{3}\right)$

_____

> **REMEMBER** The sum of additive inverses is always 0.

Simplify each expression.

3. $-6 + (-195) + 0 + 6$

_____

4. $23.35 + (-11.05) + 20 + 1.65 + 11.05$

_____

5. $14 + 21 - 0 - 14$

_____

6. $2.22 - 3.33 + 2.28 + 3.33 + 0$

_____

7. $\frac{1}{10} + \frac{5}{12} - \frac{1}{10} + \frac{1}{12}$

_____

8. $-1\frac{1}{8} + 2\frac{2}{3} - \left(-1\frac{1}{8}\right) - \frac{1}{3}$

_____

Simplify each expression. Explain each step.

9. $32.2 - (-15.9) + 10 - 15.9 + 7.8$

_____

_____

_____

10. $-7\frac{1}{2} + 6\frac{4}{5} + 1\frac{1}{2} - 0 - 6\frac{4}{5}$

_____

_____

_____

Use the properties of operations to solve each real-world problem. Explain each step.

11. Casey's bank statement was ripped, as shown.

```
Bank Statement

Opening Balance: $0

Deposit . . . . . . . . + $144.29
Withdrawal. . . . . . . − $80.32
Deposit . . . . . . . . + $25.71
Deposit . . . . . . . . + $80.32
Withdrawal. . . . . . . − $30.00

Closing Balance:
```

What is the closing balance of Casey's bank statement?

_____

_____

_____

12. A pilot took off and brought her airplane to an elevation of 15,000 feet. Over the next 2 hours, the pilot changed the elevation of her plane several times, as listed in feet:

−2,500

+3,000

−1,000

+2,500

−3,000

What is the elevation of the pilot's plane after the 2 hours?

_____

_____

_____

Solve.

13. **CONCLUDE** What must be true about the relationship between the differences of the expressions $a - b$ and $b - a$? Explain how you know.

_____

_____

_____

14. **LIST** List several rational numbers (decimals, fractions, and mixed numbers) whose sums are whole numbers. Explain why recognizing this can save you time when adding many addends.

_____

_____

_____

Multiplying Rational Numbers

UNDERSTAND The product of any number and -1 is the opposite of the number. It does not matter if the number is an integer, a fraction, or a decimal. Remember that the opposite of 0 is 0.

Multiply groups of integers, fractions, and decimals by -1. Notice the pattern.

1

Multiply integers by -1.

$-1 \times 2 = -(1 \times 2) = -(2) = -2$

$-1 \times 1 = -(1 \times 1) = -(1) = -1$

$-1 \times 0 = -(1 \times 0) = -(0) = 0$

$-1 \times -1 = -(1 \times -1) = -(-1) = 1$

$-1 \times -2 = -(1 \times -2) = -(-2) = 2$

2

Multiply fractions by -1.

$-1 \times \frac{2}{5} = -\left(1 \times \frac{2}{5}\right) = -\left(\frac{2}{5}\right) = -\frac{2}{5}$

$-1 \times \frac{1}{5} = -\left(1 \times \frac{1}{5}\right) = -\left(\frac{1}{5}\right) = -\frac{1}{5}$

$-1 \times \frac{0}{5} = -\left(1 \times \frac{0}{5}\right) = -(0) = 0$

$-1 \times -\frac{1}{5} = -\left(1 \times -\frac{1}{5}\right) = -\left(-\frac{1}{5}\right) = \frac{1}{5}$

$-1 \times -\frac{2}{5} = -\left(1 \times -\frac{2}{5}\right) = -\left(-\frac{2}{5}\right) = \frac{2}{5}$

3

Multiply decimals by -1.

$-1 \times 0.2 = -(1 \times 0.2) = -(0.2) = -0.2$

$-1 \times 0.1 = -(1 \times 0.1) = -(0.1) = -0.1$

$-1 \times 0.0 = -(1 \times 0.0) = -(0) = 0$

$-1 \times -0.1 = -(1 \times -0.1) = -(-0.1) = 0.1$

$-1 \times -0.2 = -(1 \times -0.2) = -(-0.2) = 0.2$

▶ The multiplication pattern shows that the product of every negative number and -1 is positive. The product of every positive number and -1 is negative.

The pattern above can help us understand the rules for multiplying signed numbers:

- If two rational factors have the same sign, their product is positive.

$$(+) \cdot (+) = (+) \qquad (-) \cdot (-) = (+)$$

- If one rational factor is positive and one is negative, their product is negative.

$$(+) \cdot (-) = (-)$$

⊏ Connect

Multiply groups. Vary the number of factors. Observe the results.

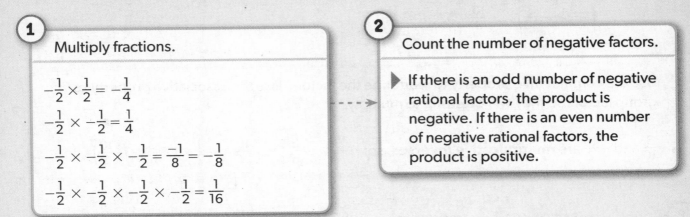

1 Multiply fractions.

$$-\frac{1}{2} \times \frac{1}{2} = -\frac{1}{4}$$

$$-\frac{1}{2} \times -\frac{1}{2} = \frac{1}{4}$$

$$-\frac{1}{2} \times -\frac{1}{2} \times -\frac{1}{2} = \frac{-1}{8} = -\frac{1}{8}$$

$$-\frac{1}{2} \times -\frac{1}{2} \times -\frac{1}{2} \times -\frac{1}{2} = \frac{1}{16}$$

2 Count the number of negative factors.

▸ If there is an odd number of negative rational factors, the product is negative. If there is an even number of negative rational factors, the product is positive.

Multiply: $1\frac{1}{4} \times -1\frac{1}{2}$

Convert the factors to improper fractions. Then multiply.

$$1\frac{1}{4} = \frac{1 \times 4 + 1}{4} = \frac{5}{4} \qquad -\left(1\frac{1}{2}\right) = -\left(\frac{1 \times 2 + 1}{2}\right) = -\left(\frac{3}{2}\right) = -\frac{3}{2}$$

$$\frac{5}{4} \times -\frac{3}{2} = \frac{5 \times (-3)}{4 \times 2} = -\frac{15}{8} = -1\frac{7}{8}$$

▸ The product is negative because the factors have opposite signs. The product is $-1\frac{7}{8}$.

Multiply: $-0.5 \times -0.4 \times -0.2$

1 Multiply one pair of factors.

$$-0.5 \times -0.4 = 0.20 = 0.2$$

The product is positive because the factors have the same sign.

2 Finish multiplying.

$$-0.5 \times -0.4 \times -0.2 = 0.2 \times -0.2$$
$$= -0.04$$

▸ The product is negative because the factors have opposite signs. The product is -0.04.

TRY

Consider multiplying 10 rational factors with these signs:
$(-) \times (-) \times (-) \times (+) \times (+) \times (-) \times (-) \times (-) \times (+) \times (+)$.
What will be the sign of the final product? Explain how you know.

EXAMPLE A Use number properties to help you multiply these three rational factors:

$$\left(-\frac{3}{7} \times -\frac{3}{10}\right) \times -\frac{10}{3}$$

1 Use the commutative property to rearrange the factors. Use the associative property to group factors so they will be easier to multiply.

$-\frac{3}{10}$ and $-\frac{10}{3}$ are **multiplicative inverses**, so: $\left(-\frac{3}{7} \times -\frac{3}{10}\right) \times -\frac{10}{3} = -\frac{3}{7} \times \left(-\frac{3}{10} \times -\frac{10}{3}\right)$

2 Use the multiplicative inverse property to simplify the expression.

$$-\frac{3}{7} \times \left(-\frac{3}{10} \times -\frac{10}{3}\right) = -\frac{3}{7} \times 1$$

3 Use the multiplicative identity property of 1.

This property states that when a number, n, is multiplied by 1, the product is the original number, n.

Therefore, $-\frac{3}{7} \times 1 = -\frac{3}{7}$.

▶ $\left(-\frac{3}{7} \times -\frac{3}{10}\right) \times -\frac{10}{3} = -\frac{3}{7}$

EXAMPLE B Solve: $0.5 \times 2.7 + 0.5 \times 5.3 - 1.2 \times 0.8$

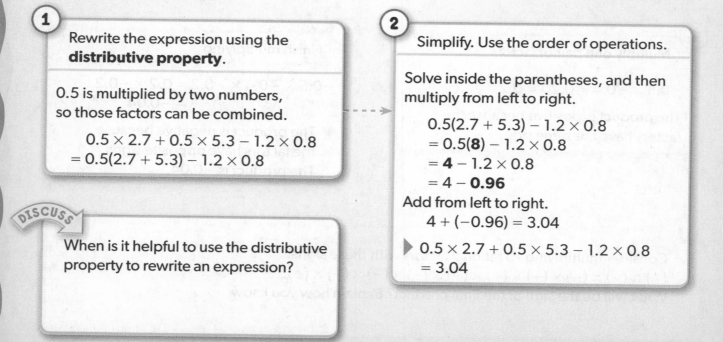

1 Rewrite the expression using the **distributive property**.

0.5 is multiplied by two numbers, so those factors can be combined.

$0.5 \times 2.7 + 0.5 \times 5.3 - 1.2 \times 0.8$
$= 0.5(2.7 + 5.3) - 1.2 \times 0.8$

DISCUSS

When is it helpful to use the distributive property to rewrite an expression?

2 Simplify. Use the order of operations.

Solve inside the parentheses, and then multiply from left to right.

$0.5(2.7 + 5.3) - 1.2 \times 0.8$
$= 0.5(\mathbf{8}) - 1.2 \times 0.8$
$= \mathbf{4} - 1.2 \times 0.8$
$= 4 - \mathbf{0.96}$

Add from left to right.
$4 + (-0.96) = 3.04$

▶ $0.5 \times 2.7 + 0.5 \times 5.3 - 1.2 \times 0.8$
$= 3.04$

⚙ Problem Solving

READ

A construction company needs to make concrete for the foundation of a building. The foundation will be 10 m long by 20 m wide by 1 m high. In order to make concrete, a mixture of cement, sand, and gravel is needed.

- The dry volume of this mixture is equal to the volume of the foundation multiplied by 1.65.
- The volume of cement is $\frac{1}{6}$ of this total volume.
- The volume of sand is $\frac{1}{3}$ of this total volume.
- The volume of gravel is $\frac{1}{2}$ of this total volume.

How much sand and gravel are needed for the construction of the foundation?

PLAN

Determine the volume of concrete needed for the foundation.

Multiply the volume of the foundation by 1.65 to find the dry volume of the mixture.

Then multiply the fractions representing the sand and gravel each by the total dry volume. Add the amounts of sand and gravel.

SOLVE

Volume of the foundation: $10 \text{ m} \times$ _____ $\times 1 \text{ m} =$ _____ m^3

Dry volume of the mixture: $1.65 \times$ _____ $=$ _____ m^3

Volume of sand: $\frac{1}{3} \times$ _____ m^3 Volume of gravel: $\frac{1}{2} \times$ _____ m^3

Volume of sand and gravel: $\left(\underline{\hspace{1cm}} \times \frac{1}{3}\right) + \left(\underline{\hspace{1cm}} \times \frac{1}{2}\right) = \underline{\hspace{1cm}} \left(\frac{1}{3} + \frac{1}{2}\right)$

Notice: We used the distributive property to determine this last expression.

Answer = _____ m^3

CHECK

Determine the volume of cement needed to make the concrete. The volume of cement subtracted from the total dry volume should match the answer.

Dry volume of the mixture: _____ m^3 Volume of cement: $\frac{1}{6} \times$ _____ $=$ _____ m^3

Difference between dry volume and cement: _____ $-$ _____ $=$ _____ m^3

➤ The combined volume of the sand and gravel needed to make the concrete for the foundation of the building is _____ m^3.

Practice

State whether the product of the factors will be *negative* or *positive*, based on the signs that are given.

1. $(+) \times (-) \times (+)$

    _____

2. $(+) \times (+) \times (+) \times (+)$

    _____

3. $(+) \times (-) \times (+) \times (-)$

    _____

> **HINT**
> What does the number of negative factors tell you about the sign of the product?

Find each product.

4. $4 \times -1 \times 9$

    _____

5. $-6 \times -5 \times -3$

    _____

6. $-\frac{1}{2} \times 10 \times -2$

    _____

7. $5.5 \times -2.4 \times 0.5 \times -0.5$

    _____

Simplify each expression. Explain which properties you used to do so.

8. $-1 \times -1 \times -1 \times -1 + 0$

    _____

    _____

9. $\left(\frac{2}{5} \times -17\right) \times \frac{5}{2}$

    _____

    _____

10. $0.1 \times 7\frac{1}{3} + 0.1 \times 2\frac{2}{3}$

    _____

    _____

11. $\left(-\frac{3}{8}\right) \times 1 \times \left(-\frac{9}{10}\right) \times -\frac{8}{3}$

    _____

    _____

For questions 12 and 13, write an expression to represent each problem. Then simplify it to answer the question.

12. Ayden has a lemonade stand. He spent $4.55 on supplies to make lemonade and $8.45 on supplies to make cookies. At his lemonade stand, he sold 23 cups of lemonade for $0.50 each and 17 cookies for $0.50 each. What were Ayden's profits that day?

    _____

13. A fish tank is shaped like a rectangular prism. Its volume can be found by multiplying the length times the width to find the area of its base, and then multiplying that area by the height. The length of the tank is $1\frac{2}{3}$ feet, its width is $\frac{3}{4}$ foot, and its height is $\frac{3}{5}$ foot. What is the volume of the fish tank, in cubic feet?

_____

Choose the best answer.

14. Which factor goes in the box to make the equation true?

$$\frac{11}{12} \times 1 \times \boxed{} = 1$$

A. $-\frac{12}{11}$ **B.** $-\frac{11}{12}$

C. $\frac{1}{12}$ **D.** $\frac{12}{11}$

15. Simplify the following expression.

$$-\frac{1}{5}\left[\frac{7}{10} + \left(-\frac{1}{5}\right)\right]$$

A. $-\frac{17}{50}$ **B.** $-\frac{1}{10}$

C. $\frac{1}{2}$ **D.** $\frac{9}{20}$

16. The signs of factors being multiplied are shown below. Which of the following would result in a product that is a positive number?

A. $(+) \cdot (+) \cdot (-)$

B. $(-) \cdot (+) \cdot (-)$

C. $(-) \cdot (-) \cdot (-)$

D. $(+) \cdot (+) \cdot (-)$

17. A rectangular frame has a length of $\frac{11}{12}$ foot and a width of $\frac{7}{12}$ foot. Which expression does **not** represent the perimeter of the frame?

A. $2\left(\frac{11}{12} + \frac{7}{12}\right)$

B. $\left(2 \times \frac{11}{12}\right) + \left(2 \times \frac{7}{12}\right)$

C. $2 + \left(\frac{11}{12} + \frac{7}{12}\right)$

D. $\frac{11}{12} + \frac{7}{12} + \frac{11}{12} + \frac{7}{12}$

Solve.

18. **EXPLAIN** Farzana knows that the additive identity property states that adding 0 to a number results in the same number. She reasons that the multiplicative identity property probably states that multiplying a number by 0 results in the same number. Is she correct? Explain.

_____

_____

19. **WRITE MATH** Ken buys 12 pencils at $0.15 each, 4 erasers at $0.15 each, and 6 pens at $0.20 each. He writes this expression to calculate his total cost, in dollars: $(0.15)(12 + 4 + 6)$. Will this expression yield the correct total cost? If not, write an accurate expression and use it to find the total cost.

_____

_____

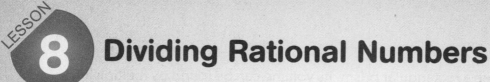

Dividing Rational Numbers

UNDERSTAND When you multiply, you can use the signs of the factors to determine the sign of the product. Similarly, when you divide, you can use the signs of the dividend and divisor to determine the sign of the quotient.

When you multiply integers, the product is always an integer. When you divide integers, however, the quotient may or may not be an integer, but it will always be a rational number that can be expressed as a fraction, as long as the divisor is not 0. Remember, a fraction with a 0 in the denominator is undefined.

Use what you know about multiplying integers to divide positive and negative integers. Notice the pattern.

Divide positive (12 and 3) and negative (-12 and -3) integers.
$12 \div 3 = 4$ because $4 \times 3 = 12$
$-12 \div 3 = -4$ because $-4 \times 3 = -12$
$12 \div (-3) = -4$ because $-4 \times (-3) = 12$
$-12 \div (-3) = 4$ because $4 \times (-3) = -12$
The quotients are integers.

Divide some other positive (2 and 5) and negative (-2 and -5) integers.
$5 \div 2 = \frac{5}{2}$ or 2.5 because $2.5 \times 2 = 5$
$-5 \div 2 = -2.5$ because $-2.5 \times 2 = -5$
$5 \div (-2) = -2.5$ because $-2.5 \times -2 = 5$
$-5 \div (-2) = 2.5$ because $2.5 \times -2 = -5$
The quotients are *not* integers, but they are rational.

Look at the patterns of the signs in each division equation. From these examples, you can deduce these rules for dividing signed numbers:

- If the divisor and dividend have the same sign, the quotient is positive.
- If the divisor and dividend have opposite signs, the quotient is negative.

◄Є Connect

Consider this statement.

If a and b are integers, then $-\left(\dfrac{a}{b}\right) = \dfrac{(-a)}{b} = \dfrac{a}{(-b)}$.

Is this statement true? Choose possible values for a and b and use them to explore this question.

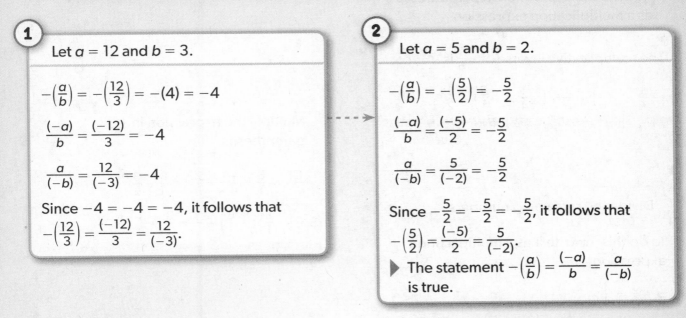

1 Let $a = 12$ and $b = 3$.

$-\left(\dfrac{a}{b}\right) = -\left(\dfrac{12}{3}\right) = -(4) = -4$

$\dfrac{(-a)}{b} = \dfrac{(-12)}{3} = -4$

$\dfrac{a}{(-b)} = \dfrac{12}{(-3)} = -4$

Since $-4 = -4 = -4$, it follows that
$-\left(\dfrac{12}{3}\right) = \dfrac{(-12)}{3} = \dfrac{12}{(-3)}$.

2 Let $a = 5$ and $b = 2$.

$-\left(\dfrac{a}{b}\right) = -\left(\dfrac{5}{2}\right) = -\dfrac{5}{2}$

$\dfrac{(-a)}{b} = \dfrac{(-5)}{2} = -\dfrac{5}{2}$

$\dfrac{a}{(-b)} = \dfrac{5}{(-2)} = -\dfrac{5}{2}$

Since $-\dfrac{5}{2} = -\dfrac{5}{2} = -\dfrac{5}{2}$, it follows that
$-\left(\dfrac{5}{2}\right) = \dfrac{(-5)}{2} = \dfrac{5}{(-2)}$.

▶ The statement $-\left(\dfrac{a}{b}\right) = \dfrac{(-a)}{b} = \dfrac{a}{(-b)}$
is true.

One way to divide rational numbers is shown above. Another way is to multiply the dividend and the multiplicative inverse (also called the **reciprocal**) of the divisor. Use some of the integers above to demonstrate this.

Divide rational numbers by multiplying the dividend and the multiplicative inverse of the divisor.

$12 \div -3 = 12 \times -\dfrac{1}{3} = -\dfrac{12}{3} = -4$

$-5 \div -2 = -5 \times -\dfrac{1}{2} = \dfrac{-5}{-2} = \dfrac{5}{2}$

▶ The examples above show another way to divide rational numbers.

TRY

Show two different ways to divide $20 \div -4$.

EXAMPLE A Solve: $\left(-\dfrac{1}{4} \div -\dfrac{1}{6}\right) \div \dfrac{3}{2}$

1

Rewrite the expression in parentheses as a multiplication expression.

The multiplicative inverse of $-\dfrac{1}{6}$ is $-\dfrac{6}{1}$, so:

$\left(-\dfrac{1}{4} \div -\dfrac{1}{6}\right) \div \dfrac{3}{2} = \left(-\dfrac{1}{4} \times -\dfrac{6}{1}\right) \div \dfrac{3}{2}.$

2

Multiply the expression in parentheses.

$-\dfrac{1}{4} \times -\dfrac{6}{1} = \dfrac{-1 \times 6}{4 \times -1} = \dfrac{-6}{-4} = \dfrac{3}{2}$

So, $\left(-\dfrac{1}{4} \times -\dfrac{6}{1}\right) \div \dfrac{3}{2} = \dfrac{3}{2} \div \dfrac{3}{2}.$

3

Divide the remaining numbers.

To do this, rewrite it as a multiplication expression.

$\dfrac{3}{2} \div \dfrac{3}{2} = \dfrac{3}{2} \times \dfrac{2}{3} = 1$

Since $\dfrac{3}{2}$ and $\dfrac{2}{3}$ are multiplicative inverses, their product is 1.

▶ $\left(-\dfrac{1}{4} \div -\dfrac{1}{6}\right) \div \dfrac{3}{2} = 1$

EXAMPLE B Solve: $(4 \div 2.5) \div 1$

1

The order of operations says to divide within the parentheses first.

$4 \div 2.5 = 1.6$

The quotient is 1.6.

2

Divide.

$(4 \div 2.5) \div 1 = 1.6 \div 1 = 1.6$ because $1.6 \times 1 = 1.6$.

▶ $(4 \div 2.5) \div 1 = 1.6$

CHECK

Use long division to check $4 \div 2.5 = 1.6$.

⚙ Problem Solving

READ

A water tank that holds 30 gallons of water when full is leaking $\frac{3}{4}$ gallon of water every hour. If no one notices and stops the leak, how many hours will it have taken for the full water tank to become empty?

PLAN

Write an equation that can be solved for the unknown, the number of hours that it will have taken before the tank is empty. Then solve the equation.

SOLVE

Let h represent the number of hours. The full water tank had 30 gallons in it. It leaks $\frac{3}{4}$ gallon every hour, which can be represented as $\frac{3}{4}h$. When the tank is empty, it will have 0 gallons in it. So the equation is $30 - \frac{3}{4}h = $ _____ .

Solve for h:

$$30 - \frac{3}{4}h = \underline{\hspace{1cm}}$$

$$30 - 30 - \frac{3}{4}h = \underline{\hspace{1cm}} - 30 \quad \text{Subtract 30 from each side.}$$

$$-\frac{3}{4}h = \underline{\hspace{1cm}}$$

To isolate the variable, h, divide $-\frac{3}{4}h$ by $-\frac{3}{4}$. To do this, multiply by the reciprocal of $-\frac{3}{4}$, which is _____ .

$$-\frac{3}{4}h \times -\frac{\square}{\square} = \underline{\hspace{1cm}} \times -\frac{\square}{\square}$$

$$h = \underline{\hspace{5cm}}$$

So, it will have taken _____ hours for the tank to become empty.

CHECK

There were 30 gallons in the full tank. If it takes _____ hours for the full tank to become empty, then you should get 30 gallons if you multiply that number of hours by $\frac{3}{4}$ gallon.

_____ hours $\times \frac{3}{4}$ gal = _____ $\times \frac{3}{4} = $ _____

▶ It will have taken _____ hours for the full water tank to become empty.

Practice

State whether the quotient will be *negative*, *positive*, *zero*, or *undefined*.

1. $(+) \div (-)$ **2.** $(-) \div 0$ **3.** $(-) \div (-)$ **4.** $0 \div (+)$

_____   _____   _____   _____

Write each quotient as a fraction.

5. $-33 \div 11$ **6.** $38 \div -29$ **7.** $-31.5 \div -4.5$ **8.** $55.25 \div 0.25$

_____   _____   _____   _____

Write *true* or *false* for each statement. If false, rewrite it so the statement is true.

9. A quotient is the result of division.

_____

10. When dividing integers, if the signs of the divisor and dividend are different, the quotient will be positive.

_____

11. One way to divide a fraction by another fraction is to multiply the dividend and the multiplicative inverse of the divisor.

_____

12. Every quotient of two integers (with a non-zero divisor) is an integer.

_____

Find each quotient. Briefly explain how you found the answer.

13. $91\frac{1}{8} \div 1$ **14.** $-0.03 \div -0.03$

_____   _____

15. $12.65 \div 1.35 \div 0 \div 0.05$ **16.** $\frac{3}{8} \div \frac{3}{8}$

_____   _____

Choose the best answer.

17. Which represents the quotient?

$$\left(-\frac{3}{5} \div 1\right) \div -\frac{5}{3}$$

A. -1

B. $-\frac{9}{25}$

C. $\frac{9}{25}$

D. 1

18. Simplify the following expression.

$$-\frac{2}{5} \div \left(\frac{8}{7} \times -\frac{7}{8}\right) \div -1$$

A. -1

B. $-\frac{2}{5}$

C. $\frac{2}{5}$

D. 1

Write an expression to represent each problem. Then simplify it.

19. The bill for a dinner was $80.00, including tax and tip. One of the diners had a coupon for $25.00 toward the dinner. The five diners then split the remaining bill equally. How much did each diner have to pay?

_____

20. A piece of wood that is 9 feet long is cut in half lengthwise. Each half is then cut lengthwise into six congruent pieces of wood. What is the length of each of the twelve small pieces of wood?

_____

Solve.

21. EXPLAIN A corporation has earned a total profit of $-\$1,419.25$ since it was founded 3.5 years ago. What is its average annual profit? Explain what this value means.

_____

_____

_____

22. SHOW Amy has $12\frac{1}{3}$ yards of fabric available to make shirts. If each shirt requires $\frac{1}{4}$ yard of fabric, how many shirts can be made? How much fabric will be left over, if any? Show your work.

_____

_____

_____

Converting Rational Numbers to Decimals

UNDERSTAND The quotient of two integers (with a non-zero divisor) is a rational number in fraction form. This means that the decimal form of the number must also be a rational number. You can tell that a decimal represents a rational number if its digits either terminate or repeat.

Find the decimal form of $\frac{7}{8}$.

Use long division.

$$
\begin{array}{r}
0.875 \\
8\overline{)7.000} \\
\end{array}
$$

$\quad -64 \quad \leftarrow 8 \times 8 = 64$

$\quad\quad 60$

$\quad -56 \quad \leftarrow 8 \times 7 = 56$

$\quad\quad 40$

$\quad -40 \quad \leftarrow 8 \times 5 = 40$

$\quad\quad\quad 0$

Because the difference is 0, the quotient terminates.

▶ The fraction $\frac{7}{8}$ is equivalent to 0.875. Both $\frac{7}{8}$ and 0.875 are rational numbers.

Find the decimal form of $\frac{5}{11}$.

Use long division.

$$
\begin{array}{r}
0.4545\ldots \\
11\overline{)5.0000} \\
\end{array}
$$

$\quad -44 \quad \leftarrow 11 \times 4 = 44$

$\quad\quad 60$

$\quad -55 \quad \leftarrow 11 \times 5 = 55$

$\quad\quad 50$

$\quad -44 \quad \leftarrow 11 \times 4 = 44$

$\quad\quad 60$

$\quad -55 \quad \leftarrow 11 \times 5 = 55$

$\quad\quad\quad 5$

Because the difference is never 0, the quotient never ends. The digits 4 and 5 repeat forever in the quotient. You can represent those repeating digits with a bar over the digits.

▶ The fraction $\frac{5}{11}$ is equivalent to $0.\overline{45}$. Both $\frac{5}{11}$ and $0.\overline{45}$ are rational numbers.

⊶€ Connect

Find the decimal form of $\frac{7}{-16}$.

Use long division.

A positive number divided by a negative number has a negative quotient.

```
        -0.4 3 7 5
 -16)7.0 0 0 0
     -6 4↓ │ │
        6 0   │ │
       -4 8↓  │ │
        1 2 0 │ │
       -1 1 2↓│
            8 0
           -8 0
              0
```
Because the difference is eventually 0, the quotient terminates.

▶ The fraction $\frac{7}{-16}$ is equivalent to -0.4375. Both $\frac{7}{-16}$ and -0.4375 are rational numbers.

Find the decimal form of $\frac{-5}{6}$.

Use long division.

```
       -0.8 3 3 3 ...
  6)-5.0 0 0 0
    -4 8↓ │ │
       2 0 │ │
      -1 8↓ │
         2 0
        -1 8↓
           2 0
          -1 8
             2
```

Because the difference continues to be 2 and will never be zero, the quotient never ends. The digit 3 repeats forever in the quotient. You can represent the repeating digit with a bar.

▶ $\frac{-5}{6} = -0.8\overline{3}$. Both $\frac{-5}{6}$ and $-0.8\overline{3}$ are rational numbers.

DISCUSS

Does the decimal form of $\frac{1}{7}$ repeat? Discuss why it may be hard to decide.

Practice

Convert each fraction to a decimal.

1. $\dfrac{2}{10}$

   $10\overline{)2}$

2. $\dfrac{4}{5}$

   $5\overline{)4}$

3. $\dfrac{1}{25}$

   $25\overline{)1}$

_____   _____   _____

> **REMEMBER** If the dividend does not have enough digits to complete the long division, insert zeros after its decimal point.

Convert each fraction to a decimal. If the decimal repeats, place a bar over the repeating digit(s).

4. $\dfrac{17}{20}$

5. $\dfrac{8}{9}$

6. $\dfrac{5}{6}$

_____   _____   _____

7. $\dfrac{3}{8}$

8. $\dfrac{1}{45}$

9. $\dfrac{-3}{16}$

_____   _____   _____

10. $\dfrac{10}{11}$

11. $\dfrac{1}{-9}$

12. $\dfrac{-14}{-15}$

_____   _____   _____

Choose the best answer.

13. What is the decimal equivalent of $\dfrac{5}{12}$?

    A. 0.416

    B. $0.\overline{416}$

    C. $0.4\overline{16}$

    D. $0.41\overline{6}$

14. What is the decimal equivalent of $\dfrac{5}{18}$?

    A. 0.2777

    B. $0.\overline{27}$

    C. $0.2\overline{7}$

    D. 0.278

Solve each problem with a decimal value.

15. Four friends earned $3 for selling seashells. To split the money evenly, they determine that each friend should receive $\frac{3}{4}$ of a dollar. How much should each friend receive? Give your answer in dollars and cents, using a decimal.

_____

16. Joey made a homemade pizza and divided it into 6 equal-sized slices. If he and his friends ate 5 of the slices, what decimal best represents the portion of the pizza that Joey and his friends ate?

_____

17. Ms. Wilson was considering buying a house, but she just learned that the average mortgage rate had increased by $\frac{1}{8}$ point. Write a decimal to represent this increase in the mortgage rate.

_____

18. Before 2000, stocks on the New York Stock Exchange were listed with fractional values. Now they are listed with decimal values to the nearest penny. In 1999, a stock's value changed by $\frac{10}{32}$. What would its change in value be, using today's value system, to the nearest penny?

_____

Solve.

19. **COMPARE** Three students represent $\frac{1}{9}$ in three different ways: 0.111..., $0.\overline{1}$, and $0.11\overline{1}$. Is there any difference in the values? Explain.

_____

_____

20. **EXPLAIN** How can you verify that a particular non-repeating decimal is the equivalent of a certain fraction? For example, verify that 0.875 is the correct decimal form of $\frac{14}{16}$. Explain your thinking.

_____

_____

_____

10 Problem Solving: Complex Fractions

Splitting Silver

READ

A jeweler has $\frac{5}{8}$ pound of silver. She wants to make pendants with 1 ounce $\left(\frac{1}{16}\text{ pound}\right)$ of silver in each. What is the maximum number of pendants she can make?

PLAN

To solve this problem, you need to divide the existing silver by the amount of silver that will be in each pendant. To divide $\frac{5}{8}$ by $\frac{1}{16}$, you can use the complex fraction $\dfrac{\frac{5}{8}}{\frac{1}{16}}$.

A complex fraction can be rewritten as a division expression: $\frac{5}{8} \div \frac{1}{16}$.

SOLVE

To divide unlike fractions, you can multiply the dividend and the reciprocal of the divisor.

The divisor is $\frac{\square}{\square}$. The reciprocal of the divisor is $\frac{\square}{\square}$. $\frac{5}{8} \div \frac{1}{16}$ becomes $\frac{5}{8} \times \frac{\square}{\square}$.

To multiply fractions, find the product of the numerators and the product of the denominators.

$$\frac{5}{8} \times \frac{16}{1} = \frac{5 \times 16}{8 \times 1} = \frac{\square}{\square} = \underline{\hspace{1.5cm}}$$

CHECK

You can check the division by using the inverse operation, $\underline{\hspace{3cm}}$.

Multiply your answer and the amount of silver in each pendant. Then check that the product is equal to the total amount of silver that the jeweler has.

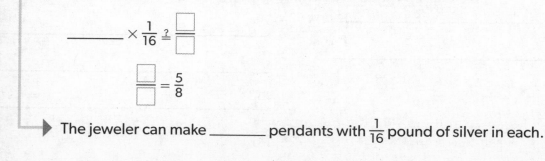

$$\underline{\hspace{1.5cm}} \times \frac{1}{16} \overset{?}{=} \frac{\square}{\square}$$

$$\frac{\square}{\square} = \frac{5}{8}$$

▶ The jeweler can make $\underline{\hspace{1.5cm}}$ pendants with $\frac{1}{16}$ pound of silver in each.

Banana Bread Loaf Recipe

READ

A recipe for a loaf of banana bread requires $\frac{3}{4}$ cup of brown sugar. Shelley has a bag with exactly $4\frac{1}{2}$ cups of brown sugar in it. What is the maximum number of loaves of banana bread that Shelley can make using her bag of brown sugar?

PLAN

To solve this problem, you need to divide the total amount of brown sugar by the amount of brown sugar used for each loaf. To divide $4\frac{1}{2}$ by $\frac{3}{4}$, you can rewrite $4\frac{1}{2}$ as

an improper fraction: $4\frac{1}{2} = \frac{4 \times 2 + 1}{2} = \frac{\square}{\square}$

Now the problem can be represented as the complex fraction $\dfrac{\square}{\frac{3}{4}}$.

SOLVE

The complex fraction represents a quotient. To divide unlike fractions, you can multiply the dividend and the reciprocal of the divisor.

The divisor is $\frac{\square}{\square}$. The reciprocal of the divisor is $\frac{\square}{\square}$. $4\frac{1}{2} \div \frac{3}{4}$ becomes $\frac{\square}{\square} \times \frac{\square}{\square}$.

To multiply fractions, find the product of the numerators and the product of the denominators.

$$\frac{9}{2} \times \frac{4}{3} = \frac{9 \times 4}{2 \times 3} = \frac{\square}{\square} = \text{_____}$$

CHECK

You can check the division by using the inverse operation, which is _____.

Multiply your answer by the amount of brown sugar used in each loaf. Then check that the product is equal to the total amount of brown sugar in Shelley's bag.

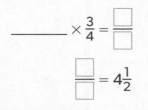

$$\text{_____} \times \frac{3}{4} = \frac{\square}{\square}$$

$$\frac{\square}{\square} = 4\frac{1}{2}$$

▶ Shelley can make _____ loaves of banana bread from $4\frac{1}{2}$ cups of brown sugar.

Practice

Use the 4-step problem-solving process to solve each problem.

1. **READ** A stack of congruent blocks, piled one on top of the other, is $\frac{4}{5}$ foot high. Each block is $\frac{1}{10}$ foot tall. How many blocks are in the stack?

   PLAN _____

   _____

   SOLVE

   CHECK

2. Abby spent $5\frac{1}{2}$ minutes solving 5 math problems on her homework. How much time did she spend on each problem, on average?

3. A piece of wire that measures $\frac{3}{4}$ inch in length is cut into shorter pieces that each measure $\frac{1}{16}$ inch. How many equal pieces are created?

4. A building has a height of $16\frac{1}{4}$ meters. Each floor in the building has a height of $3\frac{1}{4}$ meters. How many floors are in the building?

5. Three and five-sixths pounds of dirt are taken from a major-league infield. The dirt is then split into souvenir bags that contain $\frac{1}{15}$ pound each. How many bags are filled? Is there any dirt left over?

LESSON 11 Problem Solving: Rational Numbers

The Weight of Kate's Cat

READ

Kate's cat weighed $12\frac{3}{4}$ pounds at its last visit to the veterinarian. Since that visit, the cat has gained $\frac{5}{8}$ pound. How much does Kate's cat weigh now?

PLAN

To solve this problem, you need to add the $\frac{5}{8}$ pound gained to $12\frac{3}{4}$ pounds.

SOLVE

Rewrite the mixed number as an improper fraction: $12\frac{3}{4} = \dfrac{\square}{4}$

Rewrite $\dfrac{\square}{4}$ and $\dfrac{5}{8}$ as like fractions. The least common denominator of $\dfrac{5}{8}$ and $\dfrac{\square}{4}$ is _____.

Rewrite $\dfrac{\square}{4}$ as an improper fraction with a denominator of 8: $\dfrac{\square}{\square}$

To add like fractions, add the numerators and keep the denominator the same.

Rewrite your sum as a mixed number.

$\dfrac{\square}{8} + \dfrac{5}{8} = \dfrac{\square}{8} = \text{_____}\dfrac{\square}{\square}$

CHECK

You can check the addition by using the inverse operation, _____.

Subtract the amount of weight the cat gained, $\frac{5}{8}$ pound, from your answer.
The difference should be the cat's weight at the last visit, $12\frac{3}{4}$ pounds.

$$\text{_____}\dfrac{\square}{\square} - \dfrac{5}{8} \overset{?}{=} \text{_____}\dfrac{\square}{\square}$$

$$\text{_____}\dfrac{\square}{\square} = 12\frac{3}{4}$$

▶ Kate's cat now has a weight of _____ $\dfrac{\square}{\square}$ pounds.

Model Train Track Length

READ

Marko is building a model train track using wooden ties below the rails. Each tie has a width of $1\frac{1}{8}$ inches. The gap between ties is $1\frac{1}{2}$ inches. Most of the track is already in place, but Marko decides to add a section at the beginning of the track. The new section will have 20 ties and 20 gaps. What is the length of this section?

PLAN

To solve this problem, you can add the width of a tie and the width of a gap and multiply the sum by 20. You could also multiply each measure by 20.

Before you start, you need to change each mixed number to an improper fraction.

$$1\frac{1}{8} = \frac{1 \times 8 + 1}{8} = \frac{\square}{\square} \qquad 1\frac{1}{2} = \frac{1 \times 2 + 1}{2} = \frac{\square}{\square}$$

SOLVE

Write an expression to represent the situation.

20(_____ + _____)

Rewrite the expression using the distributive property. Simplify.

(_____ × _____) + (_____ × _____) = _____ + _____ = _____

CHECK

You can check the addition by solving the problem using the equivalent expression

with the distributive property: 20(_____ + _____).

Convert the fractions to like fractions and add them.

The addend $\frac{9}{8}$ will stay the same, but $\frac{\square}{\square}$ should be converted to $\frac{\square}{\square}$.

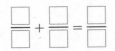

$$\frac{\square}{\square} + \frac{\square}{\square} = \frac{\square}{\square}$$

Multiply the sum by 20 and rewrite as a mixed number in simplest form:

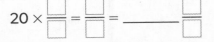

$$20 \times \frac{\square}{\square} = \frac{\square}{\square} = \_\_\_\_\_\frac{\square}{\square}$$

▶ The length of the new section of Marko's railroad track is _____ inches.

Practice

Use the 4-step problem-solving process to solve each problem.

1. **READ**   A skyscraper reaches a height of 0.15 km, including its antenna.
   The antenna has a height of 0.025 km. What is the height of the skyscraper,
   not including its antenna?

   PLAN   _____

   _____

   SOLVE

   CHECK

2. A rectangular field has dimensions of 91 feet by $60\frac{1}{3}$ feet. What is the area of the field?

3. The owner of a gas station must collect a gasoline tax of $0.12 on each gallon of gasoline sold. On Tuesday, the owner paid $264.60 in gasoline taxes. How many gallons of gasoline were sold on Tuesday?

4. The distance from the floor to the bottom of a framed painting is $3\frac{1}{4}$ feet. The height of the painting is $\frac{9}{10}$ foot. The distance from the top of the painting to the ceiling is $3\frac{1}{2}$ feet. What is the total height from the floor to the ceiling?

5. A box of nails has a mass of $\frac{7}{8}$ kilogram. Alan buys a crate of 12 of those boxes of nails. He then uses $\frac{1}{2}$ of the nails from one of the boxes. What is the total mass of the remaining nails in Alan's crate?

DOMAIN 2 Review

Choose the best answer.

1. Which decimal is equivalent to $-\frac{7}{8}$?

   A. $-0.87\overline{5}$ **B.** -0.875

   C. 0.78 **D.** 0.875

2. Which fraction does **not** represent a rational number?

   A. $-\frac{77}{78}$ **B.** $\frac{0}{25}$

   C. $\frac{-16}{-9}$ **D.** $\frac{3}{0}$

3. Which expression will result in a negative product?

   A. $(0.1)(-10)$ **B.** 0×-45

   C. $(-1)(-5)$ **D.** $-\frac{1}{2} \times 0$

4. What is the sum?

$$(7.99 + 13.22) + (-13.22)$$

   A. -7.99 **B.** 0

   C. 7.99 **D.** 21.21

5. Titan, the largest moon of Saturn, has a surface temperature of about $-178°C$. Some scientists believe this moon contains ice water. The melting temperature of water is $0°C$. By how much must the surface temperature of Titan change to melt any ice water?

   A. $-178°C$ **B.** $0°C$

   C. $178°C$ **D.** $356°C$

6. A loop around a park is $1\frac{3}{4}$ miles. If Sandy runs $\frac{2}{5}$ of the way around the loop, how far does she run?

   A. $\frac{1}{2}$ mile   **B.** $\frac{7}{10}$ mile

   C. $1\frac{3}{16}$ miles   **D.** $2\frac{3}{20}$ miles

Use the number lines to find each sum or difference.

7. $-4 + (-5) =$ _____

8. $-2 + 3 =$ _____

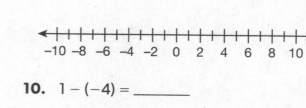

9. $7 - 9 =$ _____

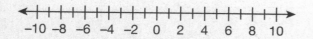

10. $1 - (-4) =$ _____

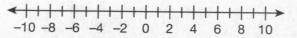

64

Rewrite each expression using the properties of operations. Then find the product or quotient.

11. $\left(\frac{3}{8} \times \frac{10}{9}\right) \times \frac{9}{10}$

_____

12. $-\frac{4}{5} \div 1 \div \frac{2}{5}$

_____

13. $-1\frac{1}{10} \times 1 \times -\frac{10}{11}$

_____

14. $0.48 \times -1.72 \times 0$

_____

Rewrite each expression as the sum of two addends. Then find the sum.

15. $-13 - 12$

_____

16. $1\frac{7}{8} - \left(-\frac{1}{8}\right)$

_____

17. $-0.03 - 1.809$

_____

Rewrite each fraction as a decimal.

18. $\frac{0}{-8} =$ _____

19. $\frac{10}{3} =$ _____

20. $\frac{-3}{-11} =$ _____

Write the value that makes the number sentence correct.

21. $77 + (-77) =$ _____

22. $-\frac{4}{15} +$ _____ $= 0$

23. _____ $+ 12.569 = 0$

The thermometer on the right shows the high and low temperatures in Liam's town one day last month. Use the thermometer for questions 24 and 25.

24. What was the range in the temperatures on that day?

_____

25. The freezing point is 32°F. How many degrees below the freezing point was the low temperature that day?

_____

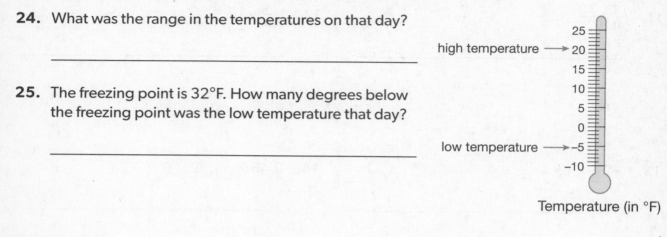

Temperature (in °F)

Solve.

26. **DESCRIBE** The following table shows the price of small, medium, and large T-shirts as well as the number of each size sold at a store one day.

Price of T-Shirts

Size	Price	Number Sold
Small	$11.25	5
Medium	$12.89	0
Large	$13.75	5

Write an expression to show the amount of money collected from selling small, medium, and large T-shirts at the store that day. Then simplify the expression to find the total amount collected. Describe any number properties you used to simplify the expression.

_____

_____

_____

27. **SHOW** Rita's baby brother weighed $7\frac{5}{16}$ pounds when he was born. Since then, her brother has gained $3\frac{3}{4}$ pounds. How much does Rita's baby brother weigh now? How could that weight be expressed as a decimal?

_____

_____

Rational Numbers Game

Materials:

Math Tool: Rational Numbers Game

two paper clips, two pencils, 3 paper bags, scrap paper

Procedure:

a. Working in pairs, cut out the numbered strips of paper and the spinners. Save the part of the page with the chart. Label each of the three bags. Label one "Integers" and put the integers strips in it. Label another bag "Fractions" and put the fraction strips in it. Label the last bag "Decimals" and put the decimal strips in it.

b. One person will spin the operations spinner while the other spins the rational numbers spinner. To do this, place a paper clip on the center of the spinner, use your pencil point to hold it in place and flick it with your finger. Choose rational numbers from the appropriate bag and use them to write two problems.

For example, if you spin "÷ and "integers", and you draw 2 and −1 from the integers bag, you would write "2 ÷ −1" and "−1 ÷ 2" as the problems. Solve the pair of problems. Notice whether or not you get the same answer.

c. On scrap paper, solve the problems. You and your partner can check each other's work.

d. After solving, record the problems and your answers in the chart. (If you run out of room in the chart, draw a new one.) Try to solve as many problems as you can in the time given. Then answer the following questions.

1. What strategies did you use to solve each of the following types of problems?

integer problems: _____

fraction problems: _____

division problems: _____

2. Did you use different strategies depending on the type of rational number? Did you use different strategies depending on the type of operation ($+$, $-$, $\times$, or $\div$)? Explain.

_____

_____

3. For some pairs of problems, you got the same answer. For some, you got different answers. What do you notice about the problems for which you got the same answer? Do they have something in common? Explain.

_____

_____

Grade 6

Grade 7

Grade 8

Grade 6 NS

Compute fluently with multi-digit numbers and find common factors and multiples.

Apply and extend previous understandings of numbers to the system of rational numbers.

Grade 6 EE

Apply and extend previous understandings of arithmetic to algebraic expressions.

Reason about and solve one-variable equations and inequalities.

Represent and analyze quantitative relationships between dependent and independent variables.

Grade 7 EE

Use properties of operations to generate equivalent expressions.

Solve real-life and mathematical problems using numerical and algebraic expressions and equations.

Grade 8 EE

Work with radicals and integer exponents.

Understand the connections between proportional relationships, lines, and linear equations.

Analyze and solve linear equations and pairs of simultaneous linear equations.

Grade 8 F

Define, evaluate, and compare functions.

Domain 3
Expressions and Equations

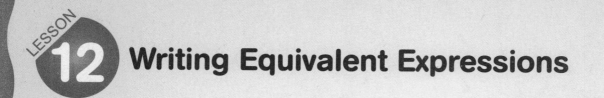

LESSON 12 Writing Equivalent Expressions

You can combine **terms** in an expression if they are **like terms**. For example, 2x and 3x are like terms. So are 5 and 7. If you had the expression $4x + 10x + 5 + 7$, you could combine 4x and 10x. You could also combine 5 and 7. You cannot combine 4x and 5 because they are not like terms.

Like terms have the same **variable**, but they do not need to have the same **coefficient**. You can use the properties of numbers to combine the coefficients of like terms.

EXAMPLE A Find the sum: $-2x + 3x$

1

Look for common factors.

Both terms have the variable, x.

So, they are like terms.

2

Use the distributive property to rewrite the expression.

$-2x + 3x$ is equal to $(-2 \cdot x) + (3 \cdot x)$.

Because x is a common factor, you can take it out of the expression.

$(-2 \cdot x) + (3 \cdot x) = x(-2 + 3)$

3

Simplify the expression.

$-2 + 3 = 1$, so $x(-2 + 3) = x(1)$.

$x(1)$ is equal to x.

▶ $-2x + 3x = x$

TRY

Simplify the expression: $7y - 2y$

EXAMPLE B Find the sum: $\left(\frac{2}{3}x + -\frac{3}{7}x\right) + \frac{3}{7}x$

1

Use number properties.

The terms $-\frac{3}{7}x$ and $\frac{3}{7}x$ are opposites. Their sum is 0. Use the associative property to group the opposites.

$\left(\frac{2}{3}x + -\frac{3}{7}x\right) + \frac{3}{7}x = \frac{2}{3}x + \left(-\frac{3}{7}x + \frac{3}{7}x\right)$

2

Simplify the expression.

Use the additive inverses and the additive identity property.

$\frac{2}{3}x + \left(-\frac{3}{7}x + \frac{3}{7}x\right) = \frac{2}{3}x + 0 = \frac{2}{3}x$

▶ $\left(\frac{2}{3}x + -\frac{3}{7}x\right) + \frac{3}{7}x = \frac{2}{3}x$

EXAMPLE C A restaurant sells sandwiches for d dollars. To keep up with rising costs, the owner will increase the price of each sandwich by 10%. Write an expression to represent the new cost of a sandwich. Then simplify it.

1

Write an expression to represent the cost of a sandwich after the increase.

Represent the current cost of a sandwich as d.

The cost, d, will be increased by 10%.

$10\% = \frac{10}{100} = 0.10 = 0.1$

So, the amount of the increase will be $0.1 \cdot d$ or $0.1d$.

The new cost will be: $d + 0.1d$.

2

Use the distributive property to rewrite the expression. Then simplify.

The terms are like terms, and the variable d is common to both terms.

$d + 0.1d = (1 \cdot d) + (0.1 \cdot d)$
$= d(1.0 + 0.1) = 1.1d$

▶ The simplified expression $1.1d$ shows the new cost of a sandwich in dollars.

DISCUSS

Suppose the restaurant owner were increasing the price of sandwiches that cost d dollars by 10 cents, instead of by 10%. Write an expression for this situation. Can you simplify the expression so that it has only one term? Explain.

Practice

State whether or not each pair of terms are like terms.

1. $-6x, 10x$

2. $3y, 6z$

3. $\frac{1}{4}k, 0.5k$

_____

_____

_____

> **HINT** If the terms have different variables, they are not like terms.

Rewrite each expression using the distributive property. Do not simplify the expression.

4. $-7x + (-2x)$

5. $y + 10y$

6. $0.2z + 1.9z$

_____

_____

_____

> **REMEMBER** When a variable is not written with a coefficient, its coefficient is 1.

Identify the property or rule that justifies each step in the calculation.

7. $4b + (-9b)$

$b(4 + -9)$ _____

$-5b$

8. $37.09m \times 1 + 0$

$37.09m + 0$ _____

$37.09m$ _____

9. $\left(-\frac{5}{6}z + \frac{1}{8}z\right) + \frac{5}{6}z$

$\left(\frac{1}{8}z + -\frac{5}{6}z\right) + \frac{5}{6}z$ _____

$\frac{1}{8}z + \left(-\frac{5}{6}z + \frac{5}{6}z\right)$ _____

$\frac{1}{8}z + 0$ _____

$\frac{1}{8}z$ _____

10. $\frac{4}{7}k + \left(j + \frac{1}{7}k\right)$

$\frac{4}{7}k + \left(\frac{1}{7}k + j\right)$ _____

$\left(\frac{4}{7}k + \frac{1}{7}k\right) + j$ _____

$k\left(\frac{4}{7} + \frac{1}{7}\right) + j$ _____

$\frac{5}{7}k + j$

Rewrite each expression using the distributive property. Then find the sum.

11. $-2.3x + (-1.7x)$

12. $\frac{3}{5}q + \left(-\frac{3}{5}q\right)$

13. $1\frac{1}{4}a + \left(-\frac{1}{4}a\right)$

_____

_____

_____

Choose the best answer.

14. What is the sum?

$3.4a + (-3.5a)$

A. $-a$ **B.** $-0.1a$

C. $0.1a$ **D.** 0

15. What is the sum?

$-3\frac{1}{3}b + b$

A. $-4\frac{1}{3}b$ **B.** $-3\frac{2}{3}b$

C. $-3b$ **D.** $-2\frac{1}{3}b$

16. A gallon of gasoline costs g dollars. Paul puts 12.5 gallons of gasoline in his car and 0.75 gallon of gasoline in a portable tank. Which shows how many dollars he spent on gasoline?

A. $13.25g$

B. $12.8g$

C. $12.5g + 0.75$

D. $12.5 + 0.75 + g$

17. Lillian buys a jacket for j dollars. She must pay 7% sales tax on her purchase. Which expression represents how many dollars she will pay in all, including sales tax?

A. $1.7j$

B. $1.07j$

C. $7j$

D. $j + 0.07$

Solve.

18. Ms. Lee sells her house for d dollars. Her real-estate agent collects a 3% commission on the sale price. Write an expression, in simplest form, to represent how many dollars Ms. Lee will receive from the sale of her house after the agent's commission is deducted from the sale price. Show or explain your work.

_____

_____

19. An electrician bought $\frac{7}{8}$ meter of copper wire from a hardware store at a cost of c dollars per meter. The electrician used $\frac{3}{4}$ meter of the copper wire for a job. Write an expression, in simplest form, to show the dollar value of the copper wire he did **not** use. Show or explain your work.

_____

_____

20. **JUSTIFY** Justify why the sum of $3a$ and $2b$ **cannot** be represented as $5ab$.

_____

_____

_____

21. **IDENTIFY** Identify the missing addend in $3.58n +$ _____ $= 0$. Explain how you determined the answer.

_____

_____

_____

13 Factoring and Expanding Linear Expressions

Expanding an expression means removing the parentheses or other grouping symbols. **Factoring** an expression means finding the **greatest common factor (GCF)** of all of the terms and then dividing each term by that factor. Factored expressions use parentheses or other grouping symbols to show what has been factored out. So, factoring an expression is the opposite of expanding it.

You can use number properties, such as the distributive property, to help you expand or factor expressions.

EXAMPLE A Expand the expression $0.4(5x + 8)$.

1

Apply the distributive property.

$0.4(5x + 8) = (0.4 \cdot 5x) + (0.4 \cdot 8)$

2

Simplify each expression in parentheses.

Since $(0.4 \cdot 5x) = 0.4 \cdot 5 \cdot x$, we can represent this as $(0.4 \cdot 5)x$.

$$(0.4 \cdot 5)x + (0.4 \cdot 8) = (2.0)x + 3.2$$
$$= 2x + 3.2$$

$2x$ and 3.2 are not like terms, so they cannot be combined.

▶ $0.4(5x + 8) = 2x + 3.2$

EXAMPLE B Expand the expression $-5(2x - 6)$.

1

Use number properties to rewrite the expression as the sum of products.

First, rewrite $2x - 6$ as an addition expression.

$-5(2x - 6) = -5[2x + (-6)]$

Apply the distributive property.

$-5[2x + (-6)] = (-5 \cdot 2x) + (-5 \cdot -6)$.

2

Simplify each expression in parentheses.

$$(-5 \cdot 2x) + (-5 \cdot -6)$$
$$= (-5 \cdot 2)x + (-5 \cdot -6) = -10x + 30$$

Because $-10x$ and 30 are not like terms, they cannot be combined.

▶ $-5(2x - 6)$ is equal to $-10x + 30$.

TRY

Expand the expression $-3(4x - 5)$.

EXAMPLE C Factor $4 + 8m$ completely.

1

Identify the GCF of the terms 4 and 8m.

The factors of 4 are 1, 2, and 4.

The term 8m is equal to $8 \cdot m$. The factors are 1, 2, 4, 8, and m.

The greatest numerical factor common to both 4 and 8m is 4.

There is no variable factor common to both 4 and 8m.

2

Use the distributive property to factor the expression.

$4 + 8m = (4 \times 1) + (4 \times 2m) = 4(1 + 2m)$

▶ The factored form of $4 + 8m$ is $4(2m + 1)$.

EXAMPLE D Factor $12n - \frac{3}{8}mn$ completely.

1

Look for the GCF of the terms 12n and $\frac{3}{8}mn$.

Since $\frac{3}{8}$ is a fraction, there is no number that can be factored from the terms.

The only factor common to both terms is the variable, n.

2

Use the distributive property to factor the expression.

$12n - \frac{3}{8}mn = (12 \times n) - \left(\frac{3}{8}m \times n\right)$

$= \left(12 - \frac{3}{8}m\right)n$

If you prefer, you could use the commutative property to rewrite the factored form as $n\left(12 - \frac{3}{8}m\right)$.

▶ The factored form of $12n - \frac{3}{8}mn$ is $n\left(12 - \frac{3}{8}m\right)$.

TRY

Factor $9x + 15y$ completely. Show your work.

Practice

Identify the GCF of each pair of terms.

1. $24y$, $36yz$

_____

2. $0.6ab$, $2b$

_____

Factor each expression completely.

3. $50x + 25$

_____

4. $16y - 12$

_____

5. $20z + 30yz$

_____

6. $21m - 35$

_____

7. $\frac{3}{4}km + 16k$

_____

8. $0.5abc - 2ac$

_____

Expand each expression.

9. $3(x + 8)$

_____

10. $4(2x - 3)$

_____

11. $\frac{1}{2}(10y + 12)$

_____

12. $-6(9z - 4)$

_____

13. $0.1(40t + 5)$

_____

14. $\frac{2}{3}\left(\frac{3}{2}x + 1\right)$

_____

Write *true* or *false* for each statement. If false, rewrite the statement so it is true.

15. Expanding an expression means removing the parentheses or grouping symbols from it.

_____

16. You can use the distributive property to help you expand and factor expressions.

_____

17. The greatest common factor of an expression can be a variable or any rational number.

_____

Choose the best answer.

18. Which expression is equivalent to $28z - 84$?

   A. $28(z + 3)$ **B.** $28(1 - 3)$

   C. $28(z - 3)$ **D.** $28z(z - 3)$

19. Which expression is equivalent to $\frac{3}{4}\left[16y - \left(-\frac{1}{2}\right)\right]$?

   A. $12y + \frac{3}{8}$ **B.** $12y + 1\frac{1}{2}$

   C. $12y - \frac{3}{8}$ **D.** $12y - 1\frac{1}{2}$

20. Kenny earns $150 for each ring he sells. He pays $85 in rent each day for his booth at a craft festival. After the cost of renting the booth is deducted, he earns $(150r - 85)$ per day. Which expression shows how many dollars he earns in 4 days at the festival?

A. 515

B. 260r

C. 600r − 85

D. 600r − 340

21. Last year, the Burrells went to the movies as a family four times and paid a total of $(8a + 12c)$ dollars for tickets for all four of those trips. Assuming they paid the same amount each time, which expression best represents how many dollars they paid each time?

A. 32a + 48c

B. 4(2a + 3c)

C. 2a + 3c

D. 2a + c

Write the property or rule that justifies each step shown.

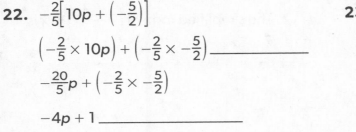

22. $-\frac{2}{5}\left[10p + \left(-\frac{5}{2}\right)\right]$

$\left(-\frac{2}{5} \times 10p\right) + \left(-\frac{2}{5} \times -\frac{5}{2}\right)$ _____

$-\frac{20}{5}p + \left(-\frac{2}{5} \times -\frac{5}{2}\right)$

$-4p + 1$ _____

23. $10c + \frac{1}{4}abc$

$(10 \times c) + \left(\frac{1}{4}ab \times c\right)$

$\left(10 + \frac{1}{4}ab\right)c$ _____

$c\left(10 + \frac{1}{4}ab\right)$ _____

Solve.

24. **SHOW** For her salary each day as a pizza delivery person, Eva earns $50 plus $2 for each pizza, p, delivered, or $(50 + 2p)$ dollars. Write an expression to show the total salary Eva will earn, in dollars, if she delivers p pizzas each day for seven days. Then expand that expression. Show or explain your work.

_____

_____

25. **COMPARE** Another pizza parlor offers Eva a job. The owner of that pizza parlor says that he will pay Eva a total of $(120 + 6p)$ dollars if she delivers p pizzas per day for 3 days. Will the new job pay more or less than her current job (described in question 24)? Use factoring to determine and explain how you made your comparison.

_____

_____

Adding and Subtracting Algebraic Expressions

EXAMPLE A Simplify: $\left(7 + \frac{1}{2}x\right) + x$

1

Use the associative property to rewrite the expression.

$\frac{1}{2}x$ and 7 are not like terms, so they cannot be added.

$\frac{1}{2}x$ and x *are* like terms. Group the like terms together.

$\left(7 + \frac{1}{2}x\right) + x = 7 + \left(\frac{1}{2}x + x\right)$

2

Use the distributive property. Combine like terms.

$7 + \left(\frac{1}{2}x + x\right)$

$= 7 + \left(\frac{1}{2} + 1\right)x$

$= 7 + \left(\frac{1}{2} + \frac{2}{2}\right)x = 7 + \frac{3}{2}x$

The terms 7 and $\frac{3}{2}x$ are not like terms, so this expression is in simplest form.

▶ The simplified form of $\left(7 + \frac{1}{2}x\right) + x$ is $7 + \frac{3}{2}x$.

EXAMPLE B Simplify: $2.5n + 9.9 - 3n$

1

Use number properties and rules to manipulate the expression.

First, rewrite the subtraction as addition.

$2.5n + 9.9 - 3n = 2.5n + 9.9 + (-3n)$

Now, use the commutative property to reorder the addends, and the associative property to group like terms.

$2.5n + 9.9 + (-3n)$

$= 2.5n + (-3n) + 9.9$

$= [2.5n + (-3n)] + 9.9$

2

Add like terms and simplify.

$[2.5n + (-3n)] + 9.9$

$= [2.5 + (-3.0)]n + 9.9$

$= -0.5n + 9.9$

▶ Since $-0.5n$ and 9.9 are not like terms, the simplest form of the expression is $-0.5n + 9.9$.

DISCUSS

Why does it help to rearrange the addends in Example B to show that $2.5n + 9.9 + (-3n)$ is equal to $2.5n + (-3n) + 9.9$?

EXAMPLE C Simplify: $\left[-\frac{7}{2}m + \left(-\frac{36}{5}\right)\right] - \frac{1}{2}m$

Use number properties and rules to manipulate the expression.

$\left[-\frac{7}{2}m + \left(-\frac{36}{5}\right)\right] - \frac{1}{2}m$

$= \left[-\frac{7}{2}m + \left(-\frac{36}{5}\right)\right] + \left(-\frac{1}{2}m\right)$ Rewrite subtraction as addition.

$= \left[-\frac{7}{2}m + \left(-\frac{1}{2}m\right)\right] + \left(-\frac{36}{5}\right)$ Use the commutative and the associative properties to rearrange and group like terms.

$= \left[-\frac{8}{2}m\right] + \left(-\frac{36}{5}\right)$ Combine like terms.

$= -4m - \frac{36}{5}$ Simplify.

▶ Since $-4m$ and $-\frac{36}{5}$ are not like terms, the simplest form of the expression is $-4m - \frac{36}{5}$.

EXAMPLE D Simplify: $5x + 3(4 - x)$

1

Use the distributive property to expand the expression.

$5x + 3(4 - x) = 5x + (3 \cdot 4) - (3 \cdot x)$
$= 5x + 12 - 3x$

2

Use number properties and rules to manipulate the expression.

Rewrite the subtraction as addition.

$5x + 12 - 3x = 5x + 12 + (-3x)$

Use the commutative property to rearrange the addends and the associative property to group like terms.

$5x + 12 + (-3x) = 5x + (-3x) + 12$
$= [5x + (-3x)] + 12$

3

Add like terms and simplify.

$[5x + (-3x)] + 12 = [5 + (-3)]x + 12$
$= (2)x + 12$
$= 2x + 12$

▶ Since $2x$ and 12 are not like terms, the simplest form of the expression is $2x + 12$.

DISCUSS

Suppose a classmate got $12 + 2x$ as the answer for Example D instead of $2x + 12$. Did your classmate give a correct answer? Explain.

Practice

For each group of three terms, identify like terms.

1. $89x, 16x, -30x$ _____

2. $2x, \frac{3}{4}z, \frac{7}{4}x$ _____

HINT: If two terms have different variables, they are not like terms.

3. $a, 0.16a, 5ab$ _____

Simplify each expression using the properties of numbers.

4. $5a + 2a + b$

_____

5. $3x + 2 + x$

_____

6. $(12y + 12) - 21y$

_____

7. $4(k + 10) + k$

_____

8. $6(p - 6) + 9p$

_____

9. $0.1t + 4.4v - 2.7t$

_____

10. $\frac{1}{2}(20m + 40) + \frac{1}{2}m$

_____

11. $\frac{13}{4}x + \frac{1}{8} - \frac{1}{2}x + \frac{3}{4}$

_____

12. $-7.6s - 1.5(8s - 20)$

_____

Simplify each expression using the properties of numbers. Show each step.

13. $12(x + 3) + 4(2x - 5)$

_____

14. $7z + 27z + 17 + 7(z - 7)$

_____

Write the property or rule that justifies each step in the calculation.

15. $17.3x + [2.7 + (-3.5x)]$

$17.3x + (-3.5x + 2.7)$ _____

$[17.3x + (-3.5x)] + 2.7$ _____

$13.8x + 2.7$

16. $2(3a + 4) + 6$

$(6a) + (2 \times 4) + 6$ _____

$6a + (8 + 6)$ _____

$6a + 14$

17. $10(3q - 2) + 20$

$10[3q + (-2)] + 20$ _____

$(10 \cdot 3q) + [10 \cdot (-2)] + 20$ _____

$30q + [(-20) + 20]$ _____

$30q$

18. $5 + (7x + 3) + (-7x)$

$5 + (3 + 7x) + (-7x)$ _____

$(5 + 3) + [7x + (-7x)]$ _____

$8 + 0$ _____

8 _____

19. $\frac{1}{2}(8 + 3x) - x$

$\left(\frac{1}{2} \cdot 8\right) + \left(\frac{1}{2} \cdot 3x\right) - x$ _____

$4 + \frac{3}{2}x - x$

$4 + \frac{3}{2}x + (-x)$ _____

$4 + \left[\frac{3}{2}x + (-x)\right]$ _____

$4 + \left[\frac{3}{2} + (-1)\right]x$ _____

$4 + \frac{1}{2}x$

20. $6b + (7c + 8b) - 9c$

$6b + (7c + 8b) + (-9c)$ _____

$6b + (8b + 7c) + (-9c)$ _____

$(6b + 8b) + [7c + (-9c)]$ _____

$(6 + 8)b + [7 + (-9)]c$ _____

$14b + (-16c)$

$14b - 16c$ _____

Solve.

21. Can $\frac{1}{2}x + \frac{2}{3}y + \frac{3}{4}$ be simplified further? Explain why or why not.

_____

_____

_____

22. What is the simplified form of $6.8x + (-8.9) + (-6.8x) + 8.9$? Explain how you know.

_____

_____

_____

23. (EXPLAIN) Explain why you should perform the distributive property in the expression $4x + 3(2x + 1)$ before simplifying it any other way. Then simplify.

_____

_____

_____

24. (RELATE) Relate what you know about simplifying expressions to what you know about factoring. For example, before you can factor $12x + 20y + y$, you need to simplify it. Explain why. Then factor it.

_____

_____

_____

Problem Solving: Algebraic Expressions and Equations

Maria's Earnings

READ

Last year, Maria earned $20 per hour at her job. This year, she received a 4% raise. How much will she earn for working a $7\frac{1}{2}$-hour day at her new pay rate?

PLAN

Translate the word problem into one or more expressions. Then simplify.

SOLVE

Convert 4% to a decimal: 4% = _____   So, the raise = 20 × _____

Her new hourly wage, in dollars, can be represented as: 20 + (20 × _____).

The amount she earns for working a $7\frac{1}{2}$-hour day can be found by multiplying that expression by $7\frac{1}{2}$. Convert $7\frac{1}{2}$ to a decimal.

$7\frac{1}{2}$ = _____

Write the complete expression below. Use the order of operations to simplify.

[20 + (20 × _____)] × _____   Multiply the terms inside the parentheses.

[20 + (_____)] × _____   Add the terms inside the grouping symbols.

_____ × _____ = _____   Multiply.

Maria will earn $_____ if she works a $7\frac{1}{2}$-hour day.

CHECK

Use mental math to check your answer.

4% of $20 is $0.80, or about $1. So, her new hourly wage is about $_____.

$7\frac{1}{2}$ hours can be rounded to a whole number of hours, _____.

Multiply the estimated wage and the estimated number of hours.

_____ × _____ = _____

Is that close to the answer you found? _____

▶ This year, Maria will earn $_____ for working a $7\frac{1}{2}$-hour day.

Hakeem's Stocks

READ

Hakeem earns money by buying and selling stocks on the stock market each day. He tracks how much money he gains or loses each day during a week. The following table shows his result, both gains and losses, each day.

Day	Monday	Tuesday	Wednesday	Thursday	Friday
Result (in US$)	145.50	−50.78	278.66	−109.22	301.19

What was the mean (average) amount of money that Hakeem earned buying and selling stocks each day during the week?

PLAN

Find the sum of all the values. Then divide by the number of values.

SOLVE

There are _____ values. Add the values.

145.50 + (−50.78) + _____ + (_____) + _____ = _____

To find the mean, divide that sum by the number of values.

_____ ÷ _____ = _____

CHECK

Use rounding to determine whether or not your answer is reasonable.

The approximate result on Monday was _____.

The approximate result on Tuesday was _____.

The approximate result on Wednesday was _____.

The approximate result on Thursday was _____.

The approximate result on Friday was _____.

The sum is _____ + _____ + _____ + _____ + _____ = _____.

The mean of the 5 rounded values is _____ ÷ _____ = _____.

Is this estimate close to the answer you found? _____

▶ Hakeem earned an average of $_____ each day by buying and selling stocks during the week.

Practice

Use the 4-step problem-solving process to solve each problem.

1. **READ**   Owen was $34\frac{1}{2}$ inches tall on his 2nd birthday. He grew an average of $2\frac{1}{2}$ inches each year for the next 10 years. Then he grew an average of $1\frac{1}{2}$ inches each year for the next 6 years. How tall was Owen on his 18th birthday?

    PLAN _____

             _____

    SOLVE

    CHECK

2.   At the beginning of the ski season on November 1, workers at a ski resort measure the height of the snow on the base of its mountain. They then measure the change in the height of the snow at the end of each month. The height of the snow on the base of the mountain at the beginning of November was 18 inches. Using the data in the table below, find the height of the snow on the base of the mountain at the end of April.

Month	Nov.	Dec.	Jan.	Feb.	Mar.	Apr.
Change in Height (in inches)	$8\frac{1}{2}$	$11\frac{1}{4}$	$20\frac{1}{2}$	10	$-12\frac{1}{2}$	$-28\frac{3}{4}$

3. The regular price of a new keyboard is $48.60. The keyboard is on sale for $\frac{1}{4}$ off. A 6% sales tax is added to the final price. What does Evan pay for the new keyboard, including sales tax? Round your answer to the nearest penny.

4. The value of a house changes each year. The following table represents the change in value each year from 2007 to 2012. Increases in value are represented by positive numbers, and decreases in value are represented by negative numbers. What was the average (mean) change in value for that six-year period? Is that average a gain or a loss in value?

Year	2007	2008	2009	2010	2011	2012
Change in Value (in US$)	4,900	3,100	−1,200	−3,800	−3,500	−2,500

5. The price of a remote-control helicopter is $34.40. A remote-control boat costs $\frac{4}{5}$ the price of the helicopter. Sales tax on the remote-control boat is 8%. What is the price of the remote-control boat, including sales tax? Round your answer to the nearest penny.

16 Word Problems with Equations

EXAMPLE A Solve for p: $4{,}450 + p = 3{,}930$

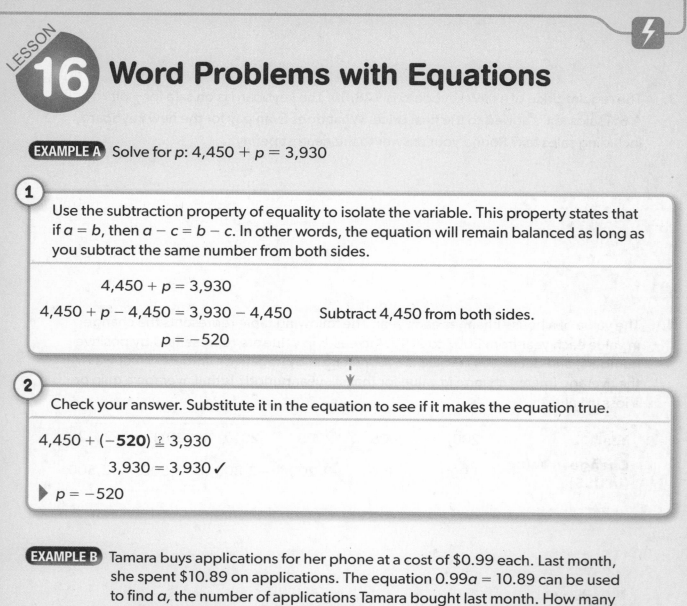

1 Use the subtraction property of equality to isolate the variable. This property states that if $a = b$, then $a - c = b - c$. In other words, the equation will remain balanced as long as you subtract the same number from both sides.

$$4{,}450 + p = 3{,}930$$
$$4{,}450 + p - 4{,}450 = 3{,}930 - 4{,}450 \quad \text{Subtract 4,450 from both sides.}$$
$$p = -520$$

2 Check your answer. Substitute it in the equation to see if it makes the equation true.

$$4{,}450 + (-\textbf{520}) \stackrel{?}{=} 3{,}930$$
$$3{,}930 = 3{,}930 ✓$$

▶ $p = -520$

EXAMPLE B Tamara buys applications for her phone at a cost of $0.99 each. Last month, she spent $10.89 on applications. The equation $0.99a = 10.89$ can be used to find a, the number of applications Tamara bought last month. How many applications did she buy last month?

1 Use the division property of equality to isolate the variable. This property states that if $a = b$ and $c \neq 0$, then $a \div c = b \div c$.

$$0.99a = 10.89$$
$$\frac{0.99a}{0.99} = \frac{10.89}{0.99} \quad \text{Divide both sides by 0.99.}$$
$$a = 11$$

2 Check your answer.

$$0.99(\textbf{11}) \stackrel{?}{=} 10.89$$
$$10.89 = 10.89 ✓$$

▶ Tamara bought 11 applications.

TRY

Solve for n: $-\frac{n}{3} = -60$. Explain how you used the multiplication property of equality to help you.

EXAMPLE C Solve for x: $\frac{1}{2}x - \frac{9}{2} = -\frac{1}{2}$

1

Get the term with the variable by itself. Use the addition property of equality, which states that if $a = b$, then $a + c = b + c$.

$\frac{1}{2}x - \frac{9}{2} = -\frac{1}{2}$

$\frac{1}{2}x - \frac{9}{2} + \frac{9}{2} = -\frac{1}{2} + \frac{9}{2}$ Add $\frac{9}{2}$ to both sides.

$\frac{1}{2}x = 4$

2

Isolate the variable. Use the multiplication property of equality, which states that if $a = b$, then $a \times c = b \times c$.

$\frac{1}{2}x \cdot \frac{2}{1} = 4 \cdot \frac{2}{1}$ Multiply both sides by 2.

$x = 8$

3

Check your answer.

$\frac{1}{2} \times \frac{8}{1} - \frac{9}{2} \overset{?}{=} -\frac{1}{2}$

$\frac{8}{2} - \frac{9}{2} \overset{?}{=} -\frac{1}{2}$

$-\frac{1}{2} = -\frac{1}{2}$ ✓

▶ $x = 8$

EXAMPLE D The cost of Judith's monthly mortgage is $900.50. She must also pay a monthly real-estate tax of q dollars. After 12 months, her total cost for the mortgage and the real-estate tax is equal to $16,401.00. This can be represented as $12(900.50 + q) = 16,401$. What is the value of q?

Get the term with the variable by itself. Then isolate the variable.

$12(900.50 + q) = 16,401$

$\dfrac{12(900.50 + q)}{12} = \dfrac{16,401}{12}$ Divide both sides by 12.

$900.50 + q = 1,366.75$

$900.50 - 900.50 + q = 1,366.75 - 900.50$ Subtract 900.50 from both sides.

$q = 466.25$

▶ The value of q is $466.25. The real-estate tax each month is $466.25.

CHECK

Show how you can check that the answer for Example D is correct.

EXAMPLE E Three more than four times a number is negative nine. What is the number?

1

Translate the words into an equation. Let *n* represent the unknown number.

Three more than four times a number is negative nine.

$$3 \quad + \quad 4 \times \quad n \quad = \quad -9$$

2

Solve for *n*.

$3 + 4n = -9$

$3 - 3 + 4n = -9 - 3$ Subtract 3 from both sides.

$4n = -12$

$\dfrac{4n}{4} = -\dfrac{12}{4}$ Divide both sides by 4.

$n = -3$

3

Use the original statement to check your answer.

Is three more than four times −**3** equal to negative nine?

Four times −3 is −12.

Three more than −12 is indeed equal to −9. ✓

▶ The number is −3.

EXAMPLE F Twice the sum of a number and negative six is four. What is the number?

1

Translate the words into an equation. Let *m* represent the unknown number.

Twice the sum of a number and negative six is four

$$2 \times \quad\quad [m \quad + \quad (-6)] \quad = \quad 4$$

2

Solve for *m*.

$2 \times [m + (-6)] = 4$

$\dfrac{2 \times [m + (-6)]}{2} = \dfrac{4}{2}$ Divide both sides by 2.

$m + (-6) = 2$

$m + (-6) + 6 = 2 + 6$ Add 6 to both sides.

$m = 8$

▶ The number is 8.

CHECK

Use the original statement to check the answer for Example F.

⚙ Problem Solving

READ

Thea bought some items using her credit card and then returned them to the store. Her credit card bill now shows that she owes −$39.98, which means that she has a credit of $39.98 on her card. She uses her card to buy 4 T-shirts, each the same price, at a store. Now her card shows that she owes $20.42. What was the price, p, of each T-shirt she bought?

PLAN

Write an equation that represents p, the price of one shirt. Then solve it for p.

SOLVE

Translate the problem into an equation.

credit of $39.98... 4 t-shirts... each the same price... would owe $20.42

$$-39.98 \quad + \quad 4 \quad \quad \times p \quad = \quad 20.42$$

This can also be written as _____ + 4p = 20.42.

Get the term with the variable by itself.

_____ + 4p = 20.42

_____ + _____ + 4p = 20.42 + _____   Add _____ to both sides.

4p = _____

Isolate the variable.

$\dfrac{4p}{4} = \dfrac{\square}{4}$ Divide both sides by _____.

$p =$ _____

CHECK

Check your answer. Substitute the value into the original problem.

The ending balance was $20.42.

Four T-shirts at $_____ each would have a total cost of 4 × $_____ = $_____.

Add that amount to $−39.98: $−39.98 + $_____ = $_____

Is the result $20.42? _____ If so, your answer is correct.

▶ Each T-shirt cost $_____.

Practice

Identify the property of equality (*addition*, *subtraction*, *multiplication*, or *division*) that could be used to isolate each variable.

1. $4x = 48$ _____

2. $k - 4.5 = 9.8$ _____

3. $\frac{n}{7} = 42$ _____

HINT — Which operation will undo the operation that is being performed on the variable?

Solve for each variable in one step.

4. $3 + x = 12$

   $x =$ _____

5. $19 + p = -8$

   $p =$ _____

6. $-3.5 + q = 14$

   $q =$ _____

7. $5x = -115$

   $x =$ _____

8. $-\frac{z}{3} = 9$

   $z =$ _____

9. $-\frac{3}{4}r = -1$

   $r =$ _____

Solve for each variable. Use more than one step. Show your work.

10. $2x + 7 = 11$

    $x =$ _____

11. $\frac{s}{5} - 3 = 2$

    $s =$ _____

12. $-6a + 10 = -27$

    $a =$ _____

13. $\frac{5}{2}b + -\frac{25}{2} = -10$

    $b =$ _____

14. $c(16 + 8.2) = -84.7$

    $c =$ _____

15. $\frac{1}{6}\left(\frac{2}{3} + d\right) = -3$

    $d =$ _____

Choose the best answer.

16. What is the value of x if $1.1(1 + x) = -99$?

    A. -91

    B. -89

    C. 89

    D. 91

17. What is the value of z if $\frac{7}{6}z + \frac{1}{3} = -\frac{5}{6}$?

    A. 1

    B. $\frac{12}{21}$

    C. 0

    D. -1

Write an equation to represent each situation. Then solve. Check your answer by substituting the value you found for the variable back into the equation you wrote.

18. The perimeter of an equilateral triangle is 21.33 centimeters. What is s, the length of each side of the triangle?

Equation: _____

19. Joy's bank account balance was $103.48. After two checks are cashed, each for the same amount, her balance is −$31.36. What is the amount, a, in dollars of each check?

Equation: _____

20. Ms. McCrory buys 12 student tickets and 12 adult tickets to a play. The total amount she pays for the tickets is $359.40. If the price of each student ticket is $10.25, what is a, the price of each adult ticket?

Equation: _____

21. In 1970, the elevation of the Dead Sea between Jordan and Israel was −1,296 feet above sea level. Since then, the elevation dropped an average of about $2\frac{1}{12}$ feet each year. How many years, y, did it take for the Dead Sea to reach an elevation of −1,371 feet above sea level?

Equation: _____

Solve.

22. **SHOW** The total charge for a taxi ride includes an initial fee of $3.25 plus $2.75 for every $\frac{1}{2}$ mile traveled. Brent took a taxi, and the ride cost him exactly $17. How many miles did he travel in the taxi? Show your work.

_____

_____

23. **COMPARE** The perimeter of a rectangle is 99 inches. Its width is 11 inches. Show how to solve for the length algebraically. Then show how to solve for the length arithmetically. Compare and contrast the solution methods. Did you get the same answer using both methods?

_____

_____

17 Word Problems with Inequalities

An **inequality** is a mathematical sentence that compares two expressions using one of these symbols: $<$ (less than), $\le$ (less than or equal to), $>$ (greater than), $\ge$ (greater than or equal to), or $\ne$ (not equal to). Solving inequalities is very similar to solving equations. However, the solution is usually a set of numbers called the **solution set**.

EXAMPLE A Solve for x: $2.5x + 4.5 > -8$

1

Isolate the variable.

$$2.5x + 4.5 > -8$$
$$2.5x + 4.5 - 4.5 > -8 - 4.5 \qquad \text{Subtract 4.5 from both sides.}$$
$$2.5x > -12.5$$
$$\frac{2.5x}{2.5} > -\frac{12.5}{2.5} \qquad \text{Divide both sides by 2.5.}$$
$$x > -5$$

2

Graph the solution set.

Any value of x that is greater than -5 is a solution to the inequality. Since -5 is *not* a solution, draw an open circle on the number line at -5. The numbers greater than -5 are to the right of -5 on the number line, so shade that part of the graph.

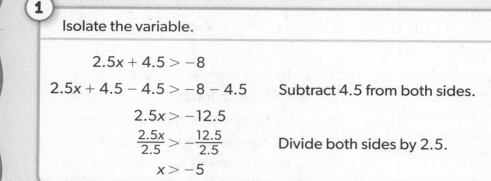

3

Check your answer. Substitute any value from the shaded part of the graph into the equation. For example, test $x = -2$.

$$2.5(-2) + 4.5 \overset{?}{>} -8$$
$$-5 + 4.5 \overset{?}{>} -8$$
$$-0.5 > -8 \checkmark$$

▶ The check shows that the solution $x > -5$ is correct.

DISCUSS

Would the graph change if the inequality symbol were $\ge$ instead of $>$? Explain.

EXAMPLE B If you multiply or divide both sides of an inequality by a negative number, you must reverse the inequality symbol.

Do you need to reverse the inequality symbol. Why or why not?

Multiply both sides of $5 > 3$ by -1.

$5 > 3$

$5(-1) > 3(-1)$

$-5 < -3$ Reverse the symbol.

▶ Since -5 is less than -3, the inequality symbol has to be reversed in order to keep the inequality true.

Divide both sides of $-6 < 5$ by -2.

$-6 < 5$

$\dfrac{-6}{-2} < \dfrac{5}{-2}$

$3 > -2\dfrac{1}{2}$ Reverse the symbol.

▶ Since 3 is greater than $-2\dfrac{1}{2}$, the inequality symbol has to be reversed.

EXAMPLE C Solve: $-x + 12 \geq 10$. Do you need to reverse the inequality symbol?

1 Isolate the variable.

$-x + 12 \geq 10$

$-x + 12 - 12 \geq 10 - 12$ Subtract 12 from both sides.

$-x \geq -2$

$\dfrac{-x}{-1} \geq \dfrac{-2}{-1}$ Divide both sides by -1.

$x \leq 2$ Reverse the symbol.

CHECK

Check that your solution, $x \leq 2$, is correct. Would it be correct if you had **not** reversed the inequality symbol?

2 Graph the solution.

Any value of x that is less than or equal to 2 is a solution to the inequality. Draw a closed circle at 2 because 2 *is* a solution. Shade the part of the number line to the left of 2.

▶ The solution set, $x \leq 2$, is graphed below.

EXAMPLE D Solve: $-4x \leq 10$

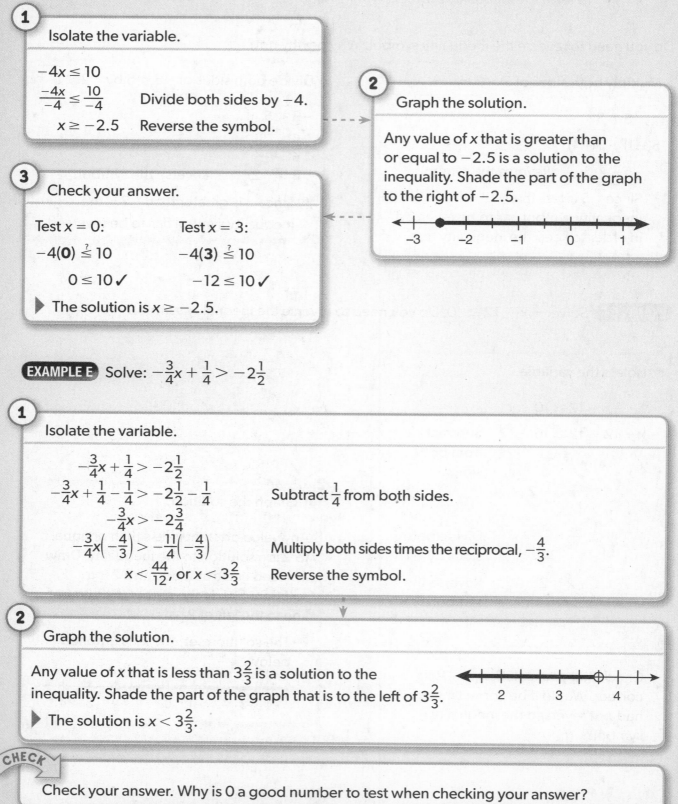

1 Isolate the variable.

$-4x \leq 10$

$\dfrac{-4x}{-4} \leq \dfrac{10}{-4}$ Divide both sides by -4.

$x \geq -2.5$ Reverse the symbol.

2 Graph the solution.

Any value of x that is greater than or equal to -2.5 is a solution to the inequality. Shade the part of the graph to the right of -2.5.

3 Check your answer.

Test $x = 0$:   Test $x = 3$:

$-4(\mathbf{0}) \overset{?}{\leq} 10$ $-4(\mathbf{3}) \overset{?}{\leq} 10$

$0 \leq 10 \checkmark$ $-12 \leq 10 \checkmark$

▶ The solution is $x \geq -2.5$.

EXAMPLE E Solve: $-\frac{3}{4}x + \frac{1}{4} > -2\frac{1}{2}$

1 Isolate the variable.

$-\frac{3}{4}x + \frac{1}{4} > -2\frac{1}{2}$

$-\frac{3}{4}x + \frac{1}{4} - \frac{1}{4} > -2\frac{1}{2} - \frac{1}{4}$ Subtract $\frac{1}{4}$ from both sides.

$-\frac{3}{4}x > -2\frac{3}{4}$

$-\frac{3}{4}x\left(-\frac{4}{3}\right) > -\frac{11}{4}\left(-\frac{4}{3}\right)$ Multiply both sides times the reciprocal, $-\frac{4}{3}$.

$x < \frac{44}{12}$, or $x < 3\frac{2}{3}$ Reverse the symbol.

2 Graph the solution.

Any value of x that is less than $3\frac{2}{3}$ is a solution to the inequality. Shade the part of the graph that is to the left of $3\frac{2}{3}$.

▶ The solution is $x < 3\frac{2}{3}$.

CHECK

Check your answer. Why is 0 a good number to test when checking your answer?

Problem Solving

READ

Ziggy earned $7.50 per hour plus an additional $100 in tips delivering pizzas on Saturday. He earned more than $145 in all. Write an inequality to show h, the number of hours he may have worked on Saturday.

PLAN

Write a(n) _____ to represent the real-world problem.

SOLVE

Translate the problem. Use h for the number of _____ that Ziggy worked.
Fill in the correct inequality symbol.

$7.50 per hour, plus, an additional $100 in tips... He earned more than $145.

$$7.50 \times \text{\_\_\_\_\_} + \qquad 100 \qquad \text{\_\_\_\_\_} \quad 145$$

Copy the inequality below and solve it.
Reverse the inequality symbol only if you multiply or divide by a _____ number.

$$7.5 \times \text{\_\_\_\_\_} + 100 \text{\_\_\_\_\_} 145$$

$$7.5h + 100 - 100 \text{\_\_\_\_\_} 145 - 100$$

$$7.5h \text{\_\_\_\_\_} 45$$

$$\frac{7.5h}{7.5} \text{\_\_\_\_\_} \frac{45}{7.5}$$

$$\text{_____}$$

The solution is h _____.
Did you reverse the inequality symbol? _____
Graph the solution set on the number line below.

$$\xleftarrow{\hspace{1cm}} \underset{0\quad1\quad2\quad3\quad4\quad5\quad6\quad7\quad8}{\rule{6cm}{0.4pt}} \xrightarrow{\hspace{1cm}}$$

CHECK

Choose two values that are part of the solution set and test them in the original inequality. Do the tested values result in a true inequality? _____

Interpret the solution in the context of the problem.

▶ Ziggy must have worked for more than _____ hours on Saturday.

Practice

Write an inequality to represent each graph.

1.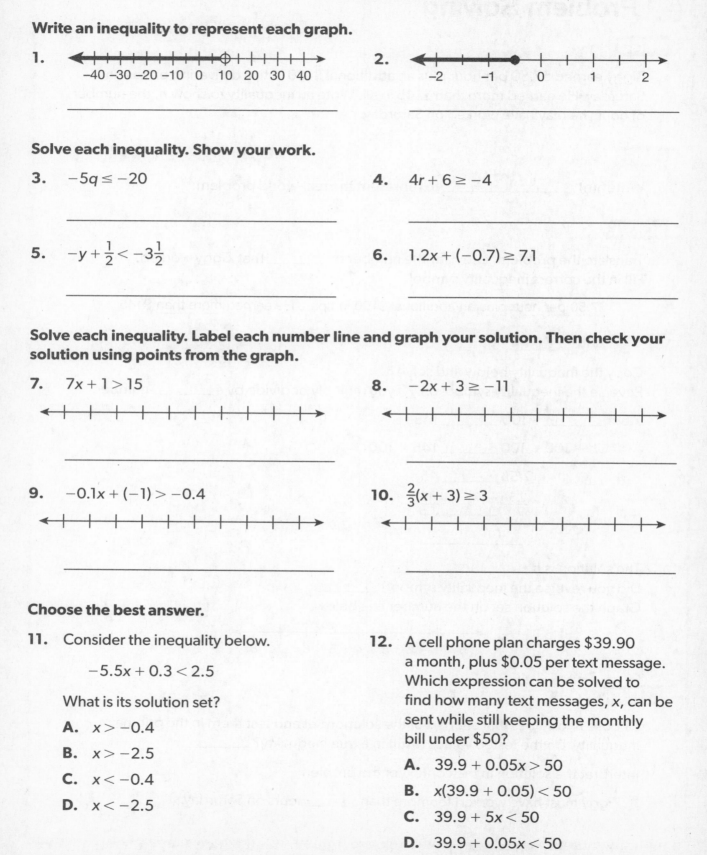

   number line: -40 -30 -20 -10 0 10 20 30 40

   _____

2. number line: -2 -1 0 1 2

   _____

Solve each inequality. Show your work.

3. $-5q \leq -20$

   _____

4. $4r + 6 \geq -4$

   _____

5. $-y + \frac{1}{2} < -3\frac{1}{2}$

   _____

6. $1.2x + (-0.7) \geq 7.1$

   _____

Solve each inequality. Label each number line and graph your solution. Then check your solution using points from the graph.

7. $7x + 1 > 15$

   number line

   _____

8. $-2x + 3 \geq -11$

   number line

   _____

9. $-0.1x + (-1) > -0.4$

   number line

   _____

10. $\frac{2}{3}(x + 3) \geq 3$

    number line

    _____

Choose the best answer.

11. Consider the inequality below.

    $$-5.5x + 0.3 < 2.5$$

    What is its solution set?

    A. $x > -0.4$

    B. $x > -2.5$

    C. $x < -0.4$

    D. $x < -2.5$

12. A cell phone plan charges $39.90 a month, plus $0.05 per text message. Which expression can be solved to find how many text messages, x, can be sent while still keeping the monthly bill under $50?

    A. $39.9 + 0.05x > 50$

    B. $x(39.9 + 0.05) < 50$

    C. $39.9 + 5x < 50$

    D. $39.9 + 0.05x < 50$

Write an inequality to represent each situation. Use _x_ for the variable. Then solve the inequality, interpreting your solution in the context of the problem.

13. A pound of seedless red grapes costs $2.75. Drew must spend less than $9.35 on a bunch of seedless red grapes.

    Inequality: _____

    Solution: _____

    Interpretation: _____

14. Chelsea earns $30 per day plus $5 for every sale that she makes at her job. On Thursday, she wants to earn at least $60.

    Inequality: _____

    Solution: _____

    Interpretation: _____

15. Mr. Mason's height is at most 4 inches more than twice his daughter's height. Mr. Mason's height is 70 inches.

    Inequality: _____

    Solution: _____

    Interpretation: _____

16. A fee of $12.50 is deducted each month from Aubryn's bank account. She currently has a balance of $75.00 in her account. She must maintain a balance greater than $0. (Assume no deposits or withdrawals.)

    Inequality: _____

    Solution: _____

    Interpretation: _____

Solve.

17. **WRITE** At most, Charlie can spend $50 on bread and turkey for a picnic. He already bought a loaf of bread for $2 and will buy turkey that costs $6 per pound. Write and solve an inequality to show how many pounds of turkey he can buy. Show your work and interpret your solution.

    _____

    _____

18. **COMPARE** How is solving an inequality similar to solving an equation? How is it different? Consider the graphing of an inequality and of an equation in your answer, and the solution or solutions you find when you solve each.

    _____

    _____

Choose the best answer.

1. Which expression is equivalent to
   $\frac{1}{3}(9g - 2)$?

   A. $3g - 2\frac{1}{3}$

   B. $3g - 2$

   C. $3g - 1\frac{2}{3}$

   D. $3g - \frac{2}{3}$

2. What is the sum?

   $[4.33a + (-4.33)] + (-1.1a)$

   A. $-1.1a$

   B. $3.23a - 4.33$

   C. $3.32a - 4.33$

   D. $5.43a + 4.33$

3. A rectangular garden has a length
   of 6.8 meters and a perimeter of
   20.6 meters. What is the width
   of the garden?

   A. 2.5 meters

   B. 3.02 meters

   C. 3.5 meters

   D. 13.8 meters

4. An actor will earn d dollars this year.
   His agent collects a commission of 10%
   of all of his earnings. Which expression
   shows how many dollars the actor
   will earn this year, after the agent's
   commission is deducted?

   A. $0.09d$

   B. $0.9d$

   C. $1.1d$

   D. $1.09d$

5. Which shows the expression
   $2ab + 6a + 12abc$ factored completely?

   A. $2a(b + 3 + 6bc)$

   B. $2(ab + 3a + 6abc)$

   C. $2a(ab + 6a + 12abc)$

   D. $20abc$

6. Solve for x: $5.1(x + 2) = 1.02$

   A. $x = -2.2$

   B. $x = -1.8$

   C. $x = 0.2$

   D. $x = 1.8$

Expand each expression.

7. $0.1(10m + 600)$

8. $\frac{3}{4}(2x - 16)$

9. $-\frac{3}{5}\left[40p + \left(-\frac{5}{3}\right)\right]$

Choose the best answer.

10. A yogurt company advertises that the capacity of its yogurt containers has increased by 20%. If the old containers had a capacity of c ounces, which expression can be used to find the capacity of the new containers?

   A. $0.20c$

   B. $1.02c$

   C. $1.2c$

   D. $21c$

11. A store must pay a credit card company $0.35 for each transaction, plus 2% of the cost of the purchase. If a customer pays for a stereo costing $180 with a credit card, how much does the store pay to the credit card company?

   A. $2.35

   B. $2.70

   C. $3.60

   D. $3.95

12. For each babysitting job she does, Emily charges $7 for each hour, x, she works plus $2 for bus fare. Emily wants to earn at least $23 for her next babysitting job. Which graph shows all the possible numbers of hours she could work and earn that amount?

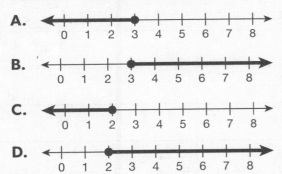

13. The high temperature in Mei's hometown was 3°C lower than twice the low temperature in her town. If the high temperature was less than 1°C, which graph could represent x, all the possible low temperatures in her town, in degrees Celsius?

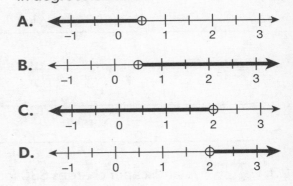

Rewrite each expression using the distributive property. Then simplify.

14. $\frac{1}{3}p + \frac{5}{3}p$

15. $4z + (-5z)$

16. $5.8y - 7.2y + 8$

Factor completely.

17. $24n + 32$

18. $\frac{5}{7}ab - 35b$

19. $100xyz - 75xy$

Choose the best answer.

20. Veronica built a shelf that is exactly $30\frac{1}{2}$ inches long. She wants to place the shelf in the center of a wall that is $60\frac{3}{4}$ inches wide. How many inches from the edge of each wall does she need to place the shelf?

A. 2 inches

B. $15\frac{1}{25}$ inches

C. $15\frac{1}{8}$ inches

D. $30\frac{1}{4}$ inches

21. Matt needs $1,800 to buy a used car. He has already saved $1,065. He earns $12.25 per hour working as a supermarket stockperson. How many hours does he need to work at his job in order to buy the car?

A. 60

B. 87

C. 147

D. 233

Solve.

22. COMPARE Tyrone works at a diner, as both a cashier and a host. He earns $7.95 per hour no matter which job he does. Tyrone wants to buy a new guitar that costs $238.50. The manager of the diner needs him to work for 18 hours next week as a cashier. If Tyrone wants to buy the guitar next week, how many hours would he need to work as a host? Solve this problem using an algebraic equation, and using an arithmetic method. Compare and contrast the sequence of operations you used in each approach. Did you get the same answer both times?

_____

_____

_____

_____

23. WRITE A landscaper charges $30 for each job, plus an additional $22.50 for each hour worked. If the landscaper charges exactly $120 for a job, write and solve an equation to determine h, the number of hours he worked during that job. How would the number sentence change if the landscaper earned *more than* $120 for the job? Use m for the number of hours he would have needed to work in that case. Solve the inequality. Then interpret it in the context of the problem.

_____

_____

_____

_____

Always, Sometimes, or Never

A variable is a letter or symbol used to represent a number. On this page, you will use shapes for variables. A negative sign in front of a shape indicates a negative variable.

Working with a partner, determine if each statement is true for all numbers, for some numbers, or for no numbers. Provide examples to support your reasoning.

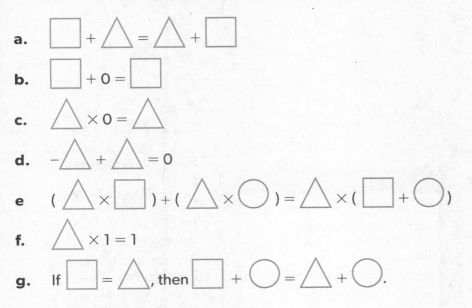

a. □ + △ = △ + □

b. □ + 0 = □

c. △ × 0 = △

d. −△ + △ = 0

e. (△ × □) + (△ × ○) = △ × (□ + ○)

f. △ × 1 = 1

g. If □ = △ , then □ + ○ = △ + ○ .

Now answer the questions below.

1. Are any of the examples above familiar to you? If so, explain.

_____

_____

2. Think of as many *different* examples as you can of statements that will *always* be true. Use variables to show them below.

Grade 6   Grade 7   Grade 8

Grade 6 NS

Compute fluently with multi-digit numbers and find common factors and multiples.

Grade 6 EE

Reason about and solve one-variable equations and inequalities.

Represent and analyze quantitative relationships between dependent and independent variables.

Grade 7 G

Draw, construct and describe geometrical figures and describe the relationships between them.

Solve real-life and mathematical problems involving angle measure, area, surface area, and volume.

Grade 8 G

Understand congruence and similarity using physical models, transparencies, or geometry software.

Understand and apply the Pythagorean Theorem.

Solve real-world and mathematical problems involving volume of cylinders, cones, and spheres.

Grade 6 G

Solve real-world and mathematical problems involving area, surface area, and volume.

Domain 4
Geometry

LESSON 18 Scale Drawings

UNDERSTAND If an object is too large or too small to draw to the correct size, it can be represented using a **scale drawing**. The drawing includes a **scale**. The scale relates the dimensions of the drawing to the dimensions of the actual object. The scale can be written as a ratio. You can then use this ratio to set up and solve a proportion to find an actual length of the object.

This drawing shows the floor plan of a room in a museum. The shape of the drawing is the same as the shape of the room. Use the scale to determine the actual length of the side of the room that is labeled z.

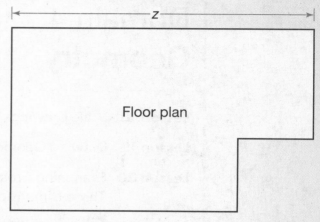

Floor plan

Scale: 0.5 cm = 1 m

1
Use a ruler to measure the length of the side labeled z on the drawing.

The side labeled z measures 8 centimeters.

2
Set up a proportion.

Use the scale shown on the drawing, 0.5 cm = 1 m, as one ratio. Write the other ratio using the scale-drawing length, 8 cm, and the variable z to represent the actual length.

$$\frac{0.5 \text{ cm}}{1 \text{ m}} = \frac{8 \text{ cm}}{z}$$

3
Solve for z.

$$\frac{0.5}{1} = \frac{8}{z}$$

$$0.5 \cdot z = 1 \cdot 8$$

$$0.5z = 8$$

$$\frac{0.5z}{0.5} = \frac{8}{0.5}$$

$$z = 16$$

▶ The actual length of the room is 16 meters.

⊸ Connect

A rectangular field has dimensions of 32 meters and 26 meters. If you wanted to create a scale drawing using the scale 0.5 cm = 1 m, what would the dimensions of the scale drawing be?

1

Instead of writing a proportion, write the proportional relationship as an equation.

Think of the scale, 0.5 cm = 1 m, as a unit rate.

So, the constant of proportionality is 0.5.

The equation is $y = 0.5x$, where x is the length of the actual object in meters and y is the length of the scale drawing in centimeters.

2

Find the scale length when the actual length is 32 meters.

$y = 0.5x$

$y = 0.5 \cdot 32$

$y = 16$

3

Find the scale width when the actual width is 26 meters.

$y = 0.5x$

$y = 0.5 \cdot 26$

$y = 13$

▶ The dimensions of the scale drawing would be 16 centimeters by 13 centimeters.

CHECK

Set up and solve proportions to check that the dimensions found above are correct. Show your work.

EXAMPLE A Lucia drew this scale drawing to show the triangular flower bed she wants to build in her yard.

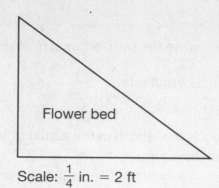

Flower bed

Scale: $\frac{1}{4}$ in. = 2 ft

Based on the drawing, what will be the area of the actual flower bed?

1

Use a ruler to measure the lengths of the base and height of the drawing.

The base of the triangle measures 2 inches. The height measures $1\frac{1}{2}$ inches.

2

Set up and solve proportions to find the actual base length, b, and height, h.

$$\frac{\frac{1}{4}}{2} = \frac{2}{b}$$ $$\frac{\frac{1}{4}}{2} = \frac{\frac{3}{2}}{h}$$

$$\frac{1}{4} \cdot b = 2 \cdot 2$$ $$\frac{1}{4} \cdot h = 2 \cdot \frac{3}{2}$$

$$\frac{b}{4} = 4$$ $$\frac{h}{4} = 3$$

$$\frac{b}{4} \cdot 4 = 4 \cdot 4$$ $$\frac{h}{4} \cdot 4 = 3 \cdot 4$$

$$b = 16 \text{ ft}$$ $$h = 12 \text{ ft}$$

3

From *Math Tool: Area Formulas (Polygons)*

Area of a triangle $= \frac{1}{2}bh$

Calculate the area: $A = \frac{1}{2} \cdot 16 \cdot 12$
$$= 8 \cdot 12 = 96 \text{ ft}^2$$

▶ The area of the triangular flower bed will be 96 square feet.

TRY

Based on the drawing, what will be the perimeter of the actual flower bed? Explain and/or show your work.

EXAMPLE B The blueprint at the right shows a rectangular classroom. The length of the scale drawing is 3 inches, and the width is 2 inches. The scale is shown.

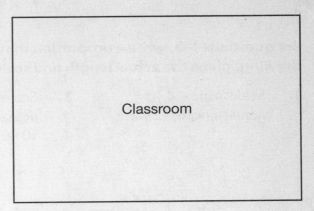

Classroom

Scale: 1 in. = 10 ft

Use a ruler to draw a blueprint of the same classroom, but use a different scale: $\frac{1}{4}$ inch = 5 feet.

1

Use proportions to determine the actual length, L, and width, W, of the classroom.

$\dfrac{1\text{ in.}}{10\text{ ft}} = \dfrac{3\text{ in.}}{L\text{ ft}}$

$\dfrac{1}{10} = \dfrac{3}{L}$

$1 \cdot L = 10 \cdot 3$

$L = 30$

$\dfrac{1\text{ in.}}{10\text{ ft}} = \dfrac{2\text{ in.}}{W\text{ ft}}$

$\dfrac{1}{10} = \dfrac{2}{W}$

$1 \cdot W = 10 \cdot 2$

$W = 20$

The actual classroom is 30 feet long and 20 feet wide.

2

Find the scale length and scale width of a drawing using this scale: $\frac{1}{4}$ inch = 5 feet.

Find the scale length, l.

$\dfrac{\frac{1}{4}\text{ in.}}{5\text{ ft}} = \dfrac{l\text{ in.}}{30\text{ ft}}$

$\dfrac{\frac{1}{4}}{5} = \dfrac{l}{30}$

$\dfrac{1}{4} \cdot 30 = 5 \cdot l$

$7.5 = 5l$

$\dfrac{7.5}{5} = \dfrac{5l}{5}$

$1.5 = l$

$\dfrac{\frac{1}{4}\text{ in.}}{5\text{ ft}} = \dfrac{w\text{ in.}}{20\text{ ft}}$

$\dfrac{\frac{1}{4}}{5} = \dfrac{w}{20}$

$\dfrac{1}{4} \cdot 20 = 5 \cdot w$

$5 = 5w$

$\dfrac{5}{5} = \dfrac{5w}{5}$

$1 = w$

The drawing will be $1\frac{1}{2}$ inches long and 1 inch wide.

3

Create the drawing.

Classroom

Scale: $\frac{1}{4}$ in. = 5 ft

▶ The drawing is shown above.

DISCUSS

Are the two blueprints the same shape? Are they the same size? Use one or two sentences to compare and contrast them.

Practice

For questions 1–3, write a proportion that could be used to find the length of a scale drawing, given the actual length and scale.

1. Scale: 1 in. = 4 yd
actual length: 12 yards

2. Scale: 3 cm = 5 mm
actual length:
10 millimeters

3. Scale: 0.5 cm = 12 km
actual length:
6 kilometers

_____   _____   _____

> REMEMBER A ratio can be
> used to represent each scale.

For questions 4 and 5, use a ruler to measure the dimensions of the drawing. Then find the actual dimensions of the object it represents. Show your work.

4.

Pool

Scale: 0.25 cm = 1 m

5.

Tabletop

Scale: $\frac{1}{2}$ in. = 1 yd

_____   _____

> 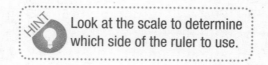 HINT Look at the scale to determine
> which side of the ruler to use.

Choose the best answer.

6. Each side of a square rug is 12 feet long.
If you create a scale drawing for the rug
using the scale 2 in. = 3 ft, how long
will each side of the drawing be?

A. 4 inches   **B.** 6 inches

C. 8 inches   **D.** 18 inches

7. A scale drawing of a rectangular field
is 10 centimeters by 8.5 centimeters.
If the actual field has dimensions of
40 meters by 34 meters, which could
be the scale used for the drawing?

A. 0.5 cm = 16 m   **B.** 0.5 cm = 8 m

C. 0.5 cm = 4 m   **D.** 0.5 cm = 2 m

Use the map and a ruler for questions 8–10. Show your work.

Town Map

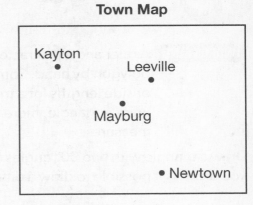

Scale: 0.5 cm = 2 km

8. Determine the actual straight-line distance between Leeville and Mayburg. _____

9. Determine the actual straight-line distance between Kayton and Leeville. _____

10. According to the map, which two towns are separated by a straight-line distance of 16 kilometers? _____

Solve. Use a ruler as needed.

11. This drawing shows a wooden, triangular deck to be built at a water park. What will the area of the actual deck be?

_____

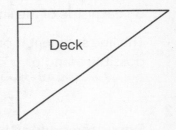

Scale: 2 cm = 5 m

12. **DEMONSTRATE** This plan shows a parking lot that will be built. How many feet of fencing are needed to surround the lot completely? Show and explain your work.

_____

Parking lot

Scale: $\frac{1}{2}$ in. = 25 ft

13. **CREATE** The scale drawing below shows a rectangular field. The scale is shown. In the space at the right, create a scale drawing for the same field, but use a different scale: 0.25 cm = 5 m. Show and explain your work.

Scale: 0.5 cm = 20 m

19 Drawing Geometric Shapes

UNDERSTAND A ruler and a protractor can help you draw a triangle or another kind of polygon by hand. Sometimes, you may be given specific angle measures or side lengths for a triangle. Determine if it is possible to draw only one unique triangle, more than one possible triangle, or no triangle with those measures.

Draw a triangle with two 60° angles and a side length of 4 centimeters. Describe the triangle you drew. Is it possible to draw a different triangle with those measures?

1

Use a ruler to draw a line segment 4 centimeters long. Then use a protractor to draw a 60° angle on each side of the line segment.

The line segment is one side of a possible triangle. The angles are two angles of a possible triangle.

2

Extend the sides of the angles until they intersect. Measure the two sides and the third angle formed. Describe the triangle.

The constructed triangle has three congruent sides, each 4 centimeters in length, and three congruent angles, each 60°.

So, it is an equilateral triangle.

3

Is it possible to draw a different triangle?

If you shorten one side of the triangle so it is shorter than 4 centimeters, the two sides will not intersect. The same is true if you extend one side of the triangle so it is longer than 4 centimeters. There is no other possible triangle with those measures.

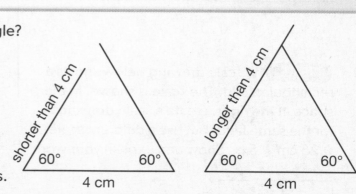

▶ The triangle has three congruent sides and three congruent angles, so it is an equilateral triangle. It is not possible to draw a different triangle.

⊸E Connect

Draw a triangle with sides 4 centimeters and 5 centimeters long and a right angle. Is it possible to draw more than one triangle with these measures?

1 Use a ruler and protractor to draw a horizontal line segment 5 centimeters long and a vertical line segment 4 centimeters long. These line segments form a 90° angle.

Connect the line segments to form a right triangle.

This right triangle has leg lengths of 4 centimeters and 5 centimeters and a hypotenuse that is approximately 6.4 centimeters long.

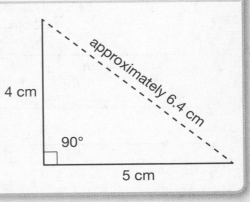

4 cm

approximately 6.4 cm

90°

5 cm

2 Try to draw a different right triangle with those side lengths.
Draw a leg that is 4 centimeters long and a short dashed ray meeting that leg at a 90° angle.

Use a ruler to draw a third side that is 5 centimeters long, using the endpoint of the 4-centimeter leg as one of its endpoints and the other endpoint intersecting the dashed ray.

This right triangle has legs that are 3 centimeters and 4 centimeters long and a hypotenuse that is 5 centimeters long.

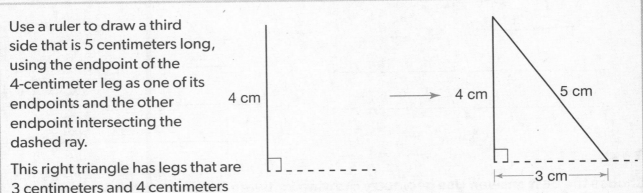

4 cm

4 cm   5 cm

3 cm

▶ It is possible to draw two different right triangles with side lengths of 4 centimeters and 5 centimeters.

MODEL

Is it possible to draw a triangle with angle measures of 30°, 40°, and 90°? Use a protractor to show why or why not.

Practice

State whether it is *possible* or *impossible* to draw a triangle with the given side lengths. Use the drawing to help you briefly explain your answer.

1. 2 centimeters, 3 centimeters, and 4 centimeters

2 cm

4 cm

_____

_____

2. 1 inch, 1 inch, and 3 inches

1 in.   1 in.

_____

_____

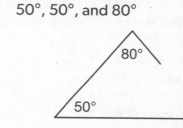

HINT

Connect the endpoints of the line segments in each drawing. Then measure the length of each side you drew.

State whether it is *possible* or *impossible* to draw a triangle with the given angle measures. Use the drawing to help you briefly explain your answer.

3. 20°, 40°, and 100°

40°

20°

_____

_____

4. 50°, 50°, and 80°

80°

50°

_____

_____

Choose the best answer. Use geometry drawing software (or a ruler, protractor, pencil, and paper) to determine the answer.

5. How many different triangles, if any, can be drawn with side lengths of 2 centimeters, 4 centimeters, and 7 centimeters?

   A. 0 triangles

   B. exactly 1 triangle

   C. exactly 2 triangles

   D. infinitely many triangles

6. How many different triangles, if any, can be drawn with one 40° angle, one 60° angle, and one 80° angle?

   A. 0 triangles

   B. exactly 1 triangle

   C. exactly 2 triangles

   D. infinitely many triangles

State whether it is possible to draw one triangle, more than one triangle, or no triangle with the given measures. On a separate sheet of paper, use a ruler and protractor to determine your answer. Draw free-hand sketches below to support your answers.

7. triangle with one 90° angle and side lengths of 5 centimeters and 12 centimeters

8. triangle with angles measuring 85° and 110° and a side length of 2 inches

10. triangle with one 100° angle and two sides measuring 1 inch each

9. triangle with one 30° angle and two sides measuring 6 centimeters each

Solve. On a separate sheet of paper, use a ruler and protractor to determine your answer. Draw free-hand sketches below to support your answers.

11. **DRAW** Ms. Lang designs custom kitchen tiles. A customer orders a set of congruent tiles shaped like parallelograms, each with a 100° angle, an 80° angle, and a side 8 inches long. Ms. Lang tells the customer that she needs more information. Use words and drawings to explain why. What additional information, if given, would allow her to design the tiles?

_____

_____

_____

12. **JUSTIFY** Jeremy makes this conjecture: The sum of the measures of the angles in a triangle is always the same number of degrees. Is his conjecture true or false? Draw several triangles and use them to justify your answer. Show your work.

_____

_____

_____

LESSON 20
Examining Cross Sections of Three-Dimensional Figures

UNDERSTAND A **three-dimensional figure** (also called a **solid figure**) has length, width, and height. **Prisms**, **pyramids**, **cylinders**, **cones**, and **spheres** are examples of three-dimensional figures.

A three-dimensional figure can be sliced by a plane to show a two-dimensional view. This view is called a **cross section**.

The three-dimensional figure on the right is a right rectangular prism with a square base. How could this prism be sliced to form the following cross sections: a square, a rectangle that is not a square, and a parallelogram that is not a rectangle?

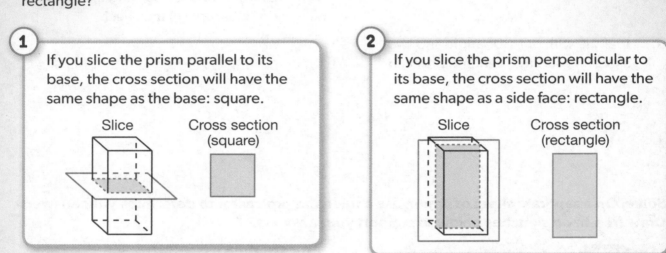

1 If you slice the prism parallel to its base, the cross section will have the same shape as the base: square.

Slice   Cross section (square)

2 If you slice the prism perpendicular to its base, the cross section will have the same shape as a side face: rectangle.

Slice   Cross section (rectangle)

3 If you slice the prism at a slant, the cross section will not have the same shape as either the base or one of the faces. It will be a parallelogram.

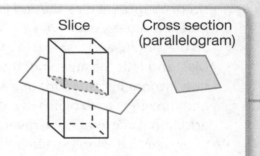

Slice   Cross section (parallelogram)

▶ The planes drawn above show how to slice the prism to form a cross section that is a square, a rectangle that is not a square, and a parallelogram that is not a rectangle.

⊸ Connect

Consider this right rectangular pyramid. What shape will the cross section be if you slice the pyramid parallel to its base? What shape will the cross section be if you slice the pyramid perpendicular to its base and through its vertex?

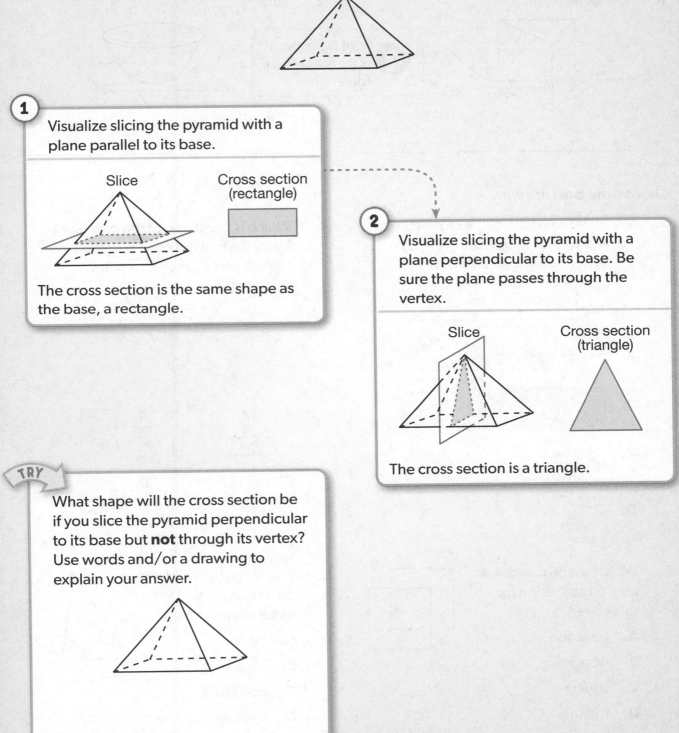

1 Visualize slicing the pyramid with a plane parallel to its base.

Slice

Cross section (rectangle)

The cross section is the same shape as the base, a rectangle.

2 Visualize slicing the pyramid with a plane perpendicular to its base. Be sure the plane passes through the vertex.

Slice

Cross section (triangle)

The cross section is a triangle.

TRY

What shape will the cross section be if you slice the pyramid perpendicular to its base but **not** through its vertex? Use words and/or a drawing to explain your answer.

Practice

Describe the shape of the cross section that is formed when the given three-dimensional figure is sliced by a plane parallel to its base.

1. triangular prism

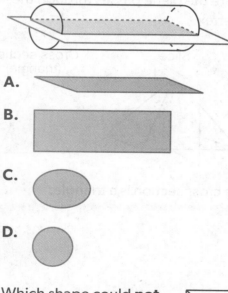

2. cone

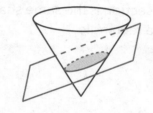

_____

Choose the best answer.

3. Which is the shape of the cross section formed when the cylinder is cut by a plane perpendicular to its base?

    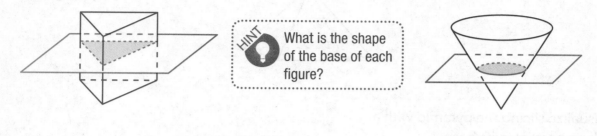

    A.

    B.

    C.

    D.

4. Which is the shape of the cross section formed when the cone is sliced by a slanted plane, as shown below?

    A. △   **B.** □

    C. ○   **D.** ⬭

5. Which shape could **not** be a cross section for this cube?

    A. hexagon

    B. octagon

    C. square

    D. triangle

6. Which shape could **not** be a cross section for this square pyramid?

    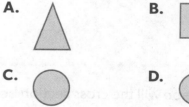

    A. circle

    B. square

    C. trapezoid

    D. triangle

Identify which two-dimensional shapes (*circle*, *ellipse*, *triangle*, *rectangle*) can be cross sections for each of the three-dimensional figures shown.

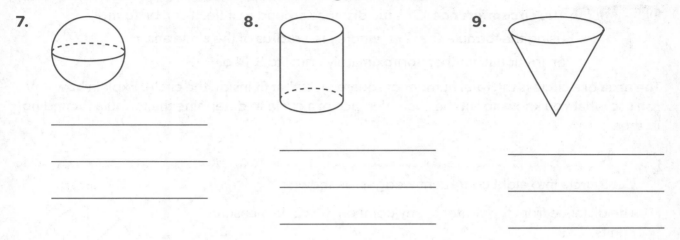

7.

_____

_____

8.

_____

_____

_____

9.

_____

_____

_____

Solve.

10. Is it possible to cut a rectangular prism so that its cross section is a circle or an ellipse? Explain your reasoning.

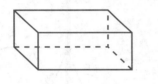

_____

_____

11. Christina molded a triangular prism from clay. She then took piano wire and sliced through the prism, as shown by the dotted lines. What is the shape of the cross section formed when she does this? Explain.

_____

12. **IDENTIFY** What solid figure has the same cross section when it is sliced by a plane parallel to its base as when it is sliced by a plane perpendicular to its base? Identify the shape of the cross section and use words and/or drawings to explain your answer.

13. **DESCRIBE** Could a three-dimensional figure with no triangular faces have a cross section that is a triangle? If so, use words and/or drawings to describe how the figure(s) could be sliced to provide that cross section.

Area and Circumference of Circles

UNDERSTAND The **circumference**, *C*, is the distance around a circle. It can be found using the formula $C = 2\pi r$, where *r* is a **radius** of the circle and π is an irrational number approximately equal to 3.14 or $\frac{22}{7}$.

The **area** of a circle is the total number of square units that fit inside the circle. Explain how you can use what you know about the circumference of a circle to determine the formula for finding its area.

1

Cut a circle into eight congruent wedges, as shown.

The distance from the center to any point on the circle measures *r* units.

The distance around the entire circle measures $2\pi r$ units. So, the distance around half the circle is equal to half of that, or πr units.

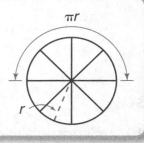

2

Visualize reassembling the wedges to look like a parallelogram.

First, rearrange them to look like a parallelogram that has a length of approximately πr units.

3

Divide one wedge in half. Move that half so the diagram resembles a rectangle.

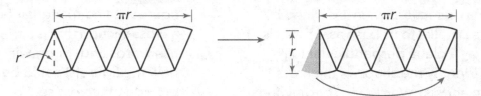

If you continue to divide the circle into congruent wedges and the number of wedges approaches infinity, the resulting figure would look more and more like a rectangle. Its length would be πr units and its width would be *r* units. So:

> *A* of circle = length × width = $\pi r \cdot r = \pi r^2$

▶ The area of a circle is found by the formula: $A = \pi r^2$.

⊏ Connect

Find the approximate circumference and area of circle O.

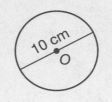

1 Determine the length of the radius of circle O.

The line segment labeled 10 cm has endpoints on the circle and passes through the center, point O. The line segment is a diameter of the circle.

The radius of a circle is equal to half its diameter, so:

$r = 10 \div 2 = 5$ cm

2 Use the formula $C = 2\pi r$ to find the approximate circumference. Use 3.14 for π.

$C = 2\pi r$

$C \approx 2 \times 3.14 \times 5$

$C \approx 31.4$ cm

Note: You are using an approximation for π, so the circumference you found, 31.4 cm, is also an approximation.

3 Use the formula $A = \pi r^2$ to find the approximate area.

$A = \pi r^2$

$A \approx 3.14 \times 5^2$

$A \approx 3.14 \times 25$

$A \approx 78.5$ cm^2

Again, 78.5 cm^2 is only an approximation of the area because you used an approximate value for π.

▶ The approximate circumference is 31.4 centimeters, and the approximate area is 78.5 square centimeters.

DISCUSS

Could you also use the formula $C = \pi d$ to find the circumference of circle O? Explain.

EXAMPLE The circumference of a circle is approximately 50.24 meters. What is its approximate area?

1

Substitute known values into the equation for the circumference of a circle.

Substitute 50.24 for C and 3.14 for π.

$C = 2\pi r$

$50.24 \approx 2 \times 3.14 \times r$

2

Solve for r.

$50.24 \approx 2 \times 3.14 \times r$

$50.24 \approx 6.28r$

$\dfrac{50.24}{6.28} \approx \dfrac{6.28r}{6.28}$

$8 \approx r$

3

Substitute that value for r in the area formula.

$A = \pi r^2$

$A \approx 3.14 \times 8^2$

$A \approx 200.96$

▶ The approximate area of the circle is 200.96 square meters.

TRY

The circumference of a circle is 28π inches. What is its radius? Show your work.

⚙ Problem Solving

READ

A circular coaster, with a diameter of 7 inches, is positioned on a white placemat. The placemat is a circle whose radius is equal to the diameter of the coaster. About how many square inches of the placemat are **not** covered by the coaster?

7 in.

PLAN

Find the area of both circles.

Then subtract the area of the _____ circle from the area of the _____ circle.

SOLVE

Find the approximate area of each circle. Use $\frac{22}{7}$ for π since the radius is a multiple of 7.

The larger circle has $r =$ _____.

A of larger circle $= \pi r^2$

$A \approx \frac{22}{7} \times ($ ___ $)^2$

$A \approx$ _____ in.^{2}

The smaller circle has $d =$ _____, so $r =$ _____.

A of smaller circle $= \pi r^2$

$A \approx \frac{22}{7} \times ($ ___ $)^2$

$A \approx$ _____ in.^{2}

Subtract to find the area of the placemat that is not covered by the coaster.

_____ − _____ = _____ in.^{2}

CHECK

Look at the diagram.

Does the smaller circle take up more than or less than $\frac{1}{2}$ of the larger circle? _____

If the fraction of the larger circle that is shaded is _____ than $\frac{1}{2}$, then I would expect that the area of the smaller circle would be _____ than half of the area of the larger circle.

$\frac{1}{2} \times$ _____ = _____

▶ The area of the smaller circle is _____ than the area of the larger circle. Since the area being subtracted from the larger circle's area is _____ than half its area, I would expect my answer to be _____ than half the area of the larger circle. My answer is _____ than half the area of the larger circle, so my answer _____ reasonable. The area of the placemat that is not covered by the coaster is about _____ in.^{2}.

Practice

A radius, *r*, or diameter, *d*, of a circle is given. Find the other measure.

1. If *d* = 4, *r* = _____.

2. If *r* = 4, *d* = _____.

3. If *d* = 3, *r* = _____.

_____   _____   _____

Find the approximate circumference of each circle shown. Show your work.

4.
5.
6.

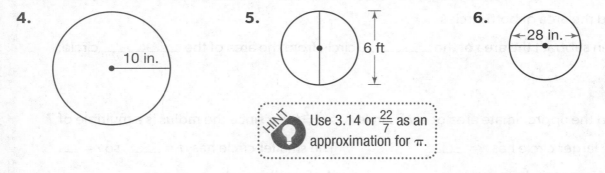

HINT Use 3.14 or $\frac{22}{7}$ as an approximation for π.

Find the approximate area of each circle shown. Show your work.

7.   2 yd
8.
9.

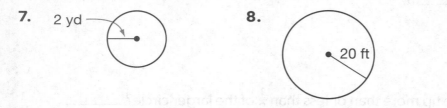   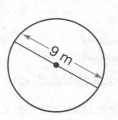

Fill in the blank with an appropriate word or phrase.

10. The radius of a circle is equal to _____ its diameter.

11. The circumference of a circle is the _____ around it.

12. The area of a circle is the number of _____ that fit inside it.

Choose the best answer.

13. Circle *A* has a circumference of 36π meters. What is the radius of circle *A*?

A. 2 m   **B.** 6 m

C. 12 m   **D.** 18 m

14. Circle *O* has a circumference of 132 feet. What is the approximate area of circle *O*?

A. 5,544 ft^2 **B.** 1,386 ft^2

C. 441 ft^2 **D.** 346.5 ft^2

Solve.

15. Jordan has a circular flower bed that is 18 feet in diameter in her yard. Approximately how many square feet of her yard is covered by the flower bed?

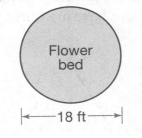

Flower bed

|← 18 ft →|

16. A circular fountain in a park is 30 feet in diameter. A park employee will plant marigolds around it. What is the circumference of the fountain?

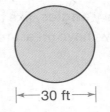

|← 30 ft →|

17. **SHOW** Two flat, circular plates are placed on a circular tabletop. The diameter of each plate equals the radius of the tabletop. How many square inches of the tabletop are **not** covered by the plates? What fraction of the tabletop is covered? Show your work.

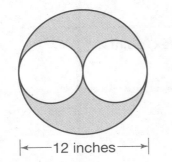

|← 12 inches →|

18. **EXPLAIN** This dartboard is divided into three regions. The outermost region has dark shading, the middle region is lightly shaded, and the center region is unshaded. What is the area of the region with the dark shading? Explain how you determined your answer.

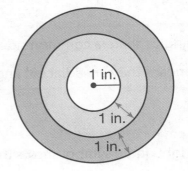

1 in.

1 in.

1 in.

22 Angle Pairs

UNDERSTAND Some pairs of angles are related in specific ways.

Adjacent angles are non-overlapping angles that share a common side and a common vertex.

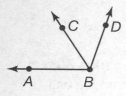

Angles *ABC* and *CBD* are adjacent.

Supplementary angles, like the pair of angles below, have measures that add to 180°.

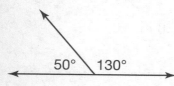

50° + 130° = 180°

Vertical angles are formed by intersecting lines and are opposite one another. They are congruent.

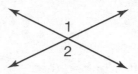

Angles 1 and 2 are vertical angles.

Complementary angles, like the pair of angles below, have measures that add to 90°.

30° + 60° = 90°

Which of the terms listed above describe angles *WXY* and *YXZ*?

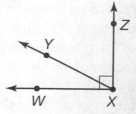

1

The angles share a common side, $\overrightarrow{XY}$, and a common vertex, point *X*.

This means they are adjacent angles.

2

The right-angle symbol shows that ∠*WXZ* measures 90°.

So, the angles that make up ∠*WXZ* are complementary angles.

▶ Angles *WXY* and *YXZ* are adjacent, complementary angles.

⤙ Connect

What is the value of x in the diagram below?

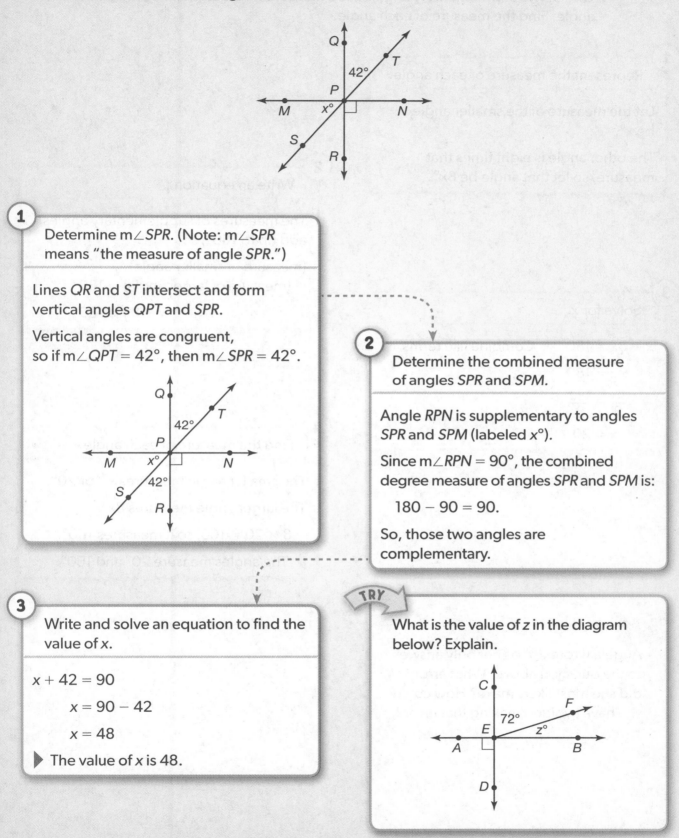

1

Determine m∠SPR. (Note: m∠SPR means "the measure of angle SPR.")

Lines QR and ST intersect and form vertical angles QPT and SPR.

Vertical angles are congruent, so if m∠QPT = 42°, then m∠SPR = 42°.

2

Determine the combined measure of angles SPR and SPM.

Angle RPN is supplementary to angles SPR and SPM (labeled x°).

Since m∠RPN = 90°, the combined degree measure of angles SPR and SPM is:

180 − 90 = 90.

So, those two angles are complementary.

3

Write and solve an equation to find the value of x.

$x + 42 = 90$

$x = 90 - 42$

$x = 48$

▶ The value of x is 48.

TRY

What is the value of z in the diagram below? Explain.

EXAMPLE One of two supplementary angles has a measure that is eight times that of the other angle. Find the measure of each angle.

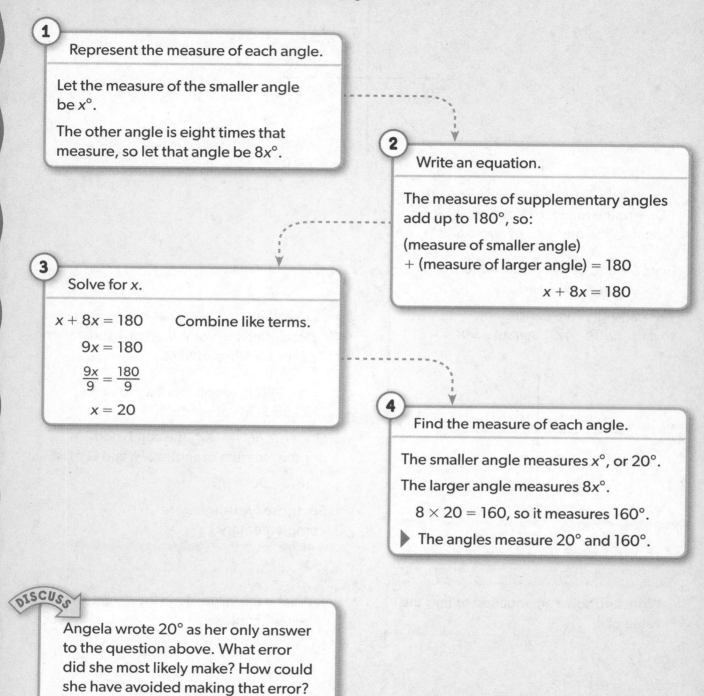

1 Represent the measure of each angle.

Let the measure of the smaller angle be $x°$.

The other angle is eight times that measure, so let that angle be $8x°$.

2 Write an equation.

The measures of supplementary angles add up to $180°$, so:

(measure of smaller angle) + (measure of larger angle) = 180

$$x + 8x = 180$$

3 Solve for x.

$x + 8x = 180$ Combine like terms.

$9x = 180$

$\dfrac{9x}{9} = \dfrac{180}{9}$

$x = 20$

4 Find the measure of each angle.

The smaller angle measures $x°$, or $20°$.

The larger angle measures $8x°$.

    $8 \times 20 = 160$, so it measures $160°$.

▶ The angles measure $20°$ and $160°$.

DISCUSS

Angela wrote $20°$ as her only answer to the question above. What error did she most likely make? How could she have avoided making that error?

⚙️ Problem Solving

READ

At the right is a diagram of a series of bike paths. The acute angle at which Paths A and B meet measures $(2x + 4)°$. The angle formed by this angle and the 56° angle measures $(4x)°$. Find and fill in the missing angle measures.

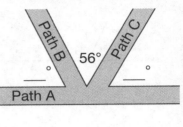

Bike Paths in Park

PLAN

Use the given information and what you know about angle pairs to find the answer.

SOLVE

Write and solve an equation:

$$(2x + 4) + (\underline{\hspace{1cm}}) = 4x$$

$$2x + \underline{\hspace{1cm}} = 4x$$

$$2x - 2x + \underline{\hspace{1cm}} = 4x - 2x$$

$$\underline{\hspace{1cm}} = 2x$$

$$\underline{\hspace{1cm}} = x$$

Find the measure of the acute angle formed by Paths A and B:

$$2x + 4 = 2(\underline{\hspace{1cm}}) + 4 = \underline{\hspace{1cm}}$$

Substitute the value of x to find the value of $4x$:

$$4x = 4(\underline{\hspace{1cm}}) = \underline{\hspace{1cm}}$$

The angles lie along a straight line, so the sum of their measures is _____°.

The acute angle at which Paths A and C meet can be represented as angle y.

Angle y is supplementary to the angle measuring $(4x)°$.

Substitute the value of $4x$ to find y: _____ + y = 180 so y = 180 − _____ = _____.

Fill in the angle measures on the diagram.

CHECK

Add the angle measures shown on the diagram. Is the sum 180°? _____

The acute angle where Path A meets Path B appears to be similar in size to the acute angle where Paths A and C meet. Are the angle measures that you wrote on the diagram close in value to one another? _____

For the reasons given above, my answer _____ reasonable.

▶ The missing angle measures are _____° and _____°.

Practice

Classify each pair of labeled angles using as many of the following terms as applicable: *adjacent*, *vertical*, *complementary*, *supplementary*.

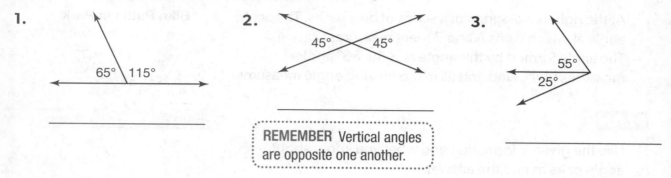

1. 65° 115°

_____

2. 45° 45°

_____

3. 55° 25°

_____

> REMEMBER Vertical angles are opposite one another.

Each pair of angle measures represents two adjacent angles. Classify each pair of angles as *complementary*, *supplementary*, or *neither*.

4. 7°, 83°

_____

5. 116°, 74°

_____

6. 90°, 90°

_____

Use the diagram on the right for questions 7–10.

7. What is the value of *a*?

_____

8. What is the value of *b*?

_____

9. What is the value of *c*?

_____

10. What is the value of *d*?

_____

$b°$ 39° $a°$ $d°$ $c°$ $d°$

Choose the best answer.

11. One of two complementary angles has a measure that is five times that of the other. Which equation could be used to find *x*, the degree measure of the smaller angle?

    A. $5x = 90$

    B. $x + 5x = 90$

    C. $5x = 180$

    D. $x + 5x = 180$

12. If one angle in a pair of vertical angles measures 42° and the other measures $(2n - 4)°$, which is the value of *n*?

    A. 42

    B. 26

    C. 23

    D. 7

Determine the value of _x_ in each diagram. Show your work.

13.

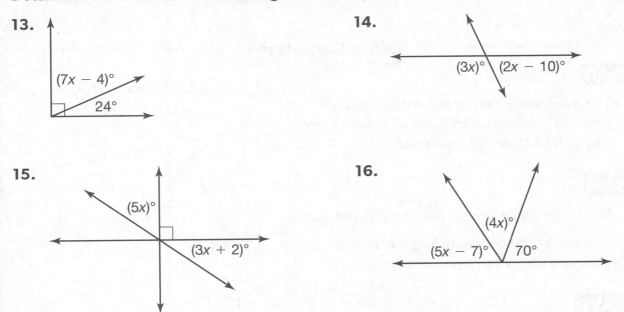

14.

15.

16.

Solve.

17. Two railroad tracks cross each other, as shown. If the measure of angle 1 is 3 times the measure of angle 2, what are the measures of angles 1, 2, 3, and 4? Explain and show your work.

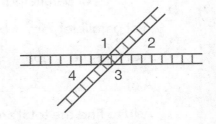

_____

_____

18. **JUSTIFY** At right are several roads that will be built as part of a new hospital complex. The angle at which Road 1 meets Road 2 is twice the measure of the angle at which Road 2 meets Road 3. Fill in the missing angle measures on the diagram. Write and solve equations to justify your answers.

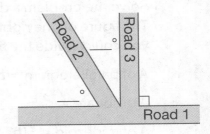

_____

_____

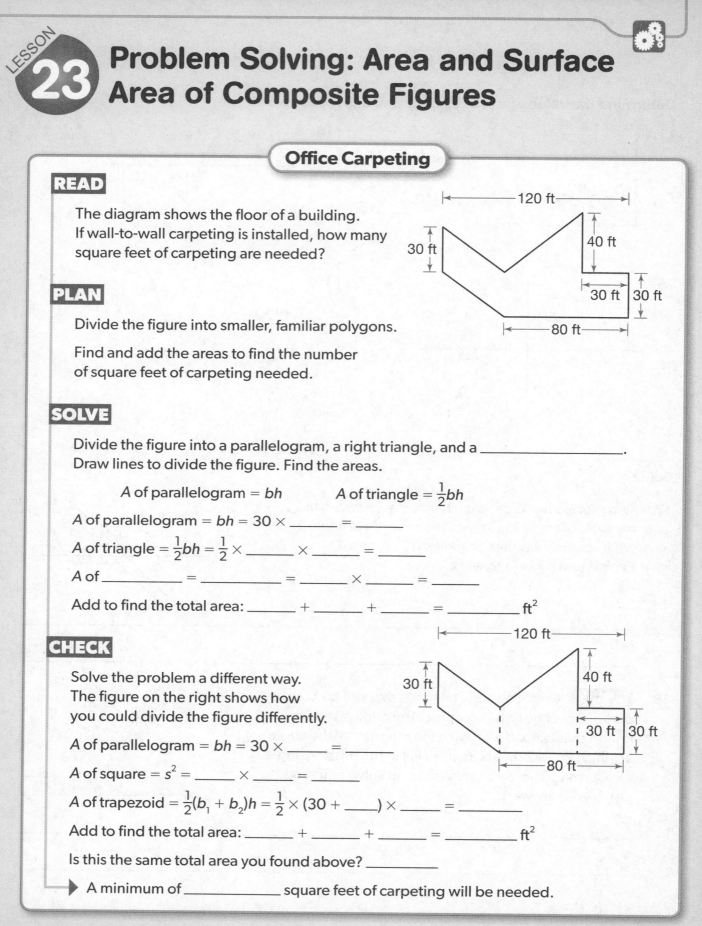

Problem Solving: Area and Surface Area of Composite Figures

LESSON 23

Office Carpeting

READ

The diagram shows the floor of a building. If wall-to-wall carpeting is installed, how many square feet of carpeting are needed?

120 ft
30 ft
40 ft
30 ft   30 ft
80 ft

PLAN

Divide the figure into smaller, familiar polygons.

Find and add the areas to find the number of square feet of carpeting needed.

SOLVE

Divide the figure into a parallelogram, a right triangle, and a _____. Draw lines to divide the figure. Find the areas.

A of parallelogram $= bh$ A of triangle $= \frac{1}{2}bh$

A of parallelogram $= bh = 30 \times$ _____ $=$ _____

A of triangle $= \frac{1}{2}bh = \frac{1}{2} \times$ _____ $\times$ _____ $=$ _____

A of _____ $=$ _____ $=$ _____ $\times$ _____ $=$ _____

Add to find the total area: _____ $+$ _____ $+$ _____ $=$ _____ ft^2

CHECK

Solve the problem a different way. The figure on the right shows how you could divide the figure differently.

120 ft
30 ft
40 ft
30 ft   30 ft
80 ft

A of parallelogram $= bh = 30 \times$ _____ $=$ _____

A of square $= s^2 =$ _____ $\times$ _____ $=$ _____

A of trapezoid $= \frac{1}{2}(b_1 + b_2)h = \frac{1}{2} \times (30 +$ ____$) \times$ ____ $=$ _____

Add to find the total area: _____ $+$ _____ $+$ _____ $=$ _____ ft^2

Is this the same total area you found above? _____

▶ A minimum of _____ square feet of carpeting will be needed.

Face Painting

READ

Karim took six congruent blocks and glued them together to make the L-shaped solid shown. The blocks are cubes with each edge measuring 3 inches. If Karim paints all the surfaces of this new figure, how many square inches will be painted?

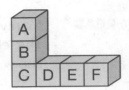

PLAN

Find the area of one face of a cube. Determine how many faces of each cube will be painted and multiply the area by that number of faces.

SOLVE

The face of a cube is a square. A of one face $= s^2 =$ _____ $\times$ _____ $=$ _____

Shade a diagram of each cube to help you determine which faces will be painted.
Cube A: 1 top face and 4 side faces painted; 5 faces total
Cube B: 4 side faces painted; 4 faces total

Cube C: _____ side faces and 1 bottom face painted; _____ faces total

Cube D: 1 top face, 1 bottom face, and _____ side faces painted; _____ faces total

Cube E: 1 top face, 1 bottom face, and _____ side faces painted; _____ faces total

Cube F: 1 _____ face, 1 _____ face, and _____ side faces painted; _____ faces total

The total number of faces shaded will be: $5 + 4 +$ _____ $+$ _____ $+$ _____ $+$ _____ $=$ _____.

Multiply that number by the area of one face: _____ $\times$ _____ $=$ _____ in.^{2}

CHECK

Check that your answer is reasonable. Find the total surface area of one cube.

SA of one cube $= 6e^2 = 6 \times ($____$)^2 =$ _____ in.^{2}

Multiply that surface area by 6, the number of cubes: $6 \times$ _____ in.$^2 =$ _____ in.^{2}.

Since not all faces will be painted, a reasonable answer will be less than the number of square inches you just found. Is your answer reasonable? _____

▶ The number of square inches of surface that will be painted is _____.

Practice

Use the 4-step problem-solving process to solve each problem.

1. **READ**   Marilyn made the figure below by gluing congruent cubes together. The length of each edge is 2 inches. What is the total surface area she would paint if she painted all the surfaces of the composite solid?

   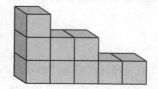

   PLAN   _____

   _____

   SOLVE

   CHECK

2. Geraldo is designing a garden in the shape of a regular hexagon with each side measuring 4 meters long. The garden will be divided into 6 equilateral triangles with a different type of flower planted in each triangle. The diagram below shows Geraldo's design. What is the approximate total area of the garden?

   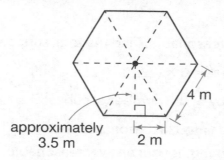

   approximately
   3.5 m   4 m   2 m

3. The floor of an art museum is shown at the right. If the entire floor is polished, how many square meters will be polished?

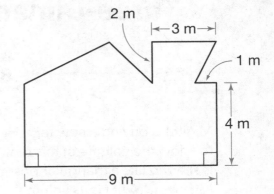

4. A cake company manufactures these special cake boxes, shaped like trapezoidal prisms. What is the minimum number of square centimeters of cardboard needed to make one of these boxes?

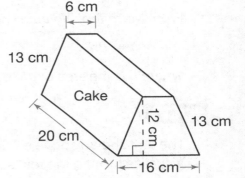

5. Morgan lines up congruent measuring blocks, each with an edge length of 5 units, to form Figure 1. She then moves the "C" block to form Figure 2. Does moving this one block increase or decrease the surface area of the composite figure? How much is the increase or decrease in surface area?

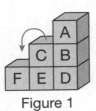

Figure 1

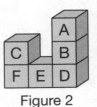

Figure 2

Problem Solving: Volume of Three-Dimensional Figures

Buying a New Tent

READ

Miguel is buying a new tent. He wants to know the volume of this tent, which is shaped like a triangular prism, before he buys it. What is its volume?

PLAN

Use the formula for finding the _____ of a prism.

From *Math Tool: Volume Formulas*

$$V = Bh$$

where B is the area of the base and h is the height.

SOLVE

The tent shown above is resting on one of its rectangular faces. Visualize turning the tent so it is resting on one of its bases. This makes it easier to see that the base of the prism is actually a _____.

Area of base, B, $= \frac{1}{2} \times$ base of triangle $\times$ height of triangle

$$= \frac{1}{2} \times \text{\_\_\_\_} \times \text{\_\_\_\_\_}$$

$$= \text{_____}$$

The height of the prism is _____.

So the volume, V, of the prism $= Bh =$ ____ $\times$ ____ $=$ _____.

CHECK

Be sure you used only the necessary information given to calculate the volume. For example, one length shown on the diagram is extraneous information that you did not need to use to find the volume. That length measures _____.

▶ The volume of the tent is _____ cubic feet.

An Arrangement of Cubes

READ

These congruent cubes have been arranged to make the figure shown below. What is the total volume of the figure?

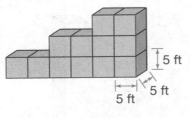

PLAN

Find the volume of one cube.

Then _____ that volume by the number of cubes.

SOLVE

The base of a cube is a square. Each edge of a cube measures _____ feet.

The area of the base of a cube = $B = s^2 =$ ____ × ____ = _____.

The volume, V, of a cube = $Bh =$ ____ × ____ = _____.

There are _____ cubes in the figure, so

V of the figure = ____ × ____ = _____.

CHECK

If you visualize moving two cubes to the left as shown, you will turn the figure into a rectangular prism. Doing this does not change the total volume of the figure because the total number of cubes does not change.

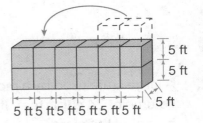

Find the volume of this prism to solve the problem a different way and check that the answer you found above is correct.

The base of the rectangular prism is a rectangle _____ feet long and 5 feet wide.

The area of the base = $B = lw =$ _____.

The height of the prism is 10 feet.

So, V of the prism = $Bh =$ ____ × ____ = _____.

Is this the same volume you found above? _____

▶ The volume of the figure is _____ cubic feet.

Practice

Use the 4-step problem-solving process to solve each problem.

1. **READ**   Carla has built the figure below using congruent cubes. What is the total volume of the figure she built?

   PLAN   _____

   _____

   SOLVE

   CHECK

2. A large crate used by a moving company is shaped like a rectangular prism and has a volume of 24 cubic feet. If the base of the crate has an area of 12 square feet, what is the height of the crate?

3. Mr. Wu bought the entertainment center shown at the right. What is the volume of the entertainment center?

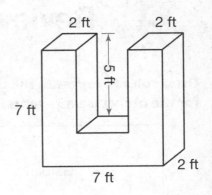

2 ft   2 ft

5 ft

7 ft

2 ft

7 ft

4. Erika made a birdhouse shaped like a pentagonal prism, as shown. What is the total volume of the birdhouse she built?

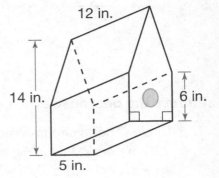

12 in.

14 in.

6 in.

5 in.

5. A swimming pool looks like a rectangle from above. However, the pool has a shallow end that is all the same depth, and a deep end that drops off, as shown. What is the maximum volume of water that the pool holds?

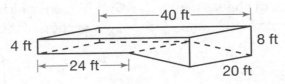

40 ft

4 ft

8 ft

24 ft

20 ft

Use a ruler to measure the dimensions of the drawing. Then find the actual dimensions for the object it represents.

1.

```
┌─────────────────────────┐
│                         │
│         Garden          │
│                         │
└─────────────────────────┘
```

Scale: 0.25 cm = 1 m

_____

2.

```
┌─────────────────────────┐
│                         │
│                         │
│      Bedroom floor      │
│                         │
│                         │
└─────────────────────────┘
```

Scale: $\frac{1}{2}$ in. = 6 ft

_____

Choose the best answer.

3. Circle *O* has a circumference of 220 meters. What is the approximate area of circle *O*?

   A. 3,850 square meters

   B. 1,225 square meters

   C. 962.5 square meters

   D. 35 square meters

4. One of a pair of vertical angles measures $(5x − 1)°$, and the other measures $(4x + 10)°$. What is the measure of each of the angles?

   A. 9°

   B. 11°

   C. 46°

   D. 54°

5. How many cubic inches of cheese can this plastic container hold?

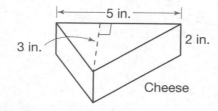

   A. 5 cubic inches

   B. 15 cubic inches

   C. 30 cubic inches

   D. $40\frac{1}{2}$ cubic inches

6. Which could **not** be the shape of a cross section of this cylinder?

   A. circle

   B. ellipse

   C. rectangle

   D. triangle

Choose the best answer.

7. A scale drawing of a rectangular field is 6 centimeters by 9 centimeters. If the actual field has dimensions of 84 meters by 126 meters, which could be the scale used for the drawing?

   A. 0.5 cm = 3.5 m

   B. 0.5 cm = 7 m

   C. 0.5 cm = 14 m

   D. 0.5 cm = 21 m

8. The dotted lines show how piano wire is used to slice this cube. What will be the shape of the cross section?

   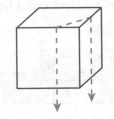

   A. trapezoid

   B. square

   C. rectangle (not a square)

   D. ellipse

Determine the value of x in each diagram.

9.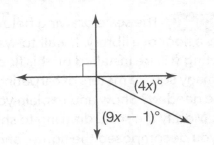

10.

Choose the best answer. Use a ruler, protractor, pencil, and paper to determine the answer.

11. How many different triangles, if any, can be drawn with one 90° angle and side lengths of 5 centimeters and 12 centimeters?

    A. 0 triangles

    B. exactly 1 triangle

    C. exactly 2 triangles

    D. infinitely many triangles

12. How many different triangles, if any, can be drawn with one 60° angle and two sides measuring 2 inches each?

    A. 0 triangles

    B. exactly 1 triangle

    C. exactly 2 triangles

    D. infinitely many triangles

Choose the best answer.

13. The congruent cubes below were glued together. If the edges of each cube measure 2 inches, what is the total surface area of the solid figure?

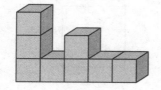

   A. 136 square inches

   B. 132 square inches

   C. 128 square inches

   D.   64 square inches

14. The congruent cubes below were glued together. If the edges of each cube measure 4 millimeters, what is the total volume of the solid figure?

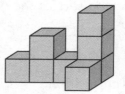

   A. 512 cubic millimeters

   B. 528 cubic millimeters

   C. 544 cubic millimeters

   D. 768 cubic millimeters

Solve. Use a ruler, if needed.

15. **DEMONSTRATE** Janna has three flat plates, each the same size. She stores them in an L-shaped drawer, as shown, so that they fit snugly inside, with no space between the edges of the drawer and the plates. Approximately how many square centimeters of the bottom of the drawer are **not** covered by plates? Show and explain your work.

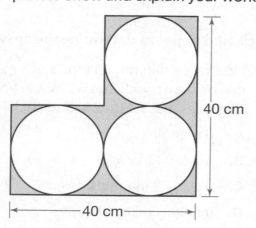

40 cm

40 cm

16. **ILLUSTRATE** The scale drawing below shows a floor of a library. If wall-to-wall carpeting will be installed on this floor, how many square meters of carpeting will be needed? Show and explain your work. Modify the scale drawing to show how you decomposed the figure, and label the actual dimensions of the parts.

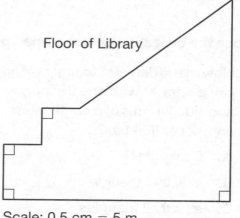

Floor of Library

Scale: 0.5 cm = 5 m

Exploring Composite Solids

Working in small groups or individually, use *Math Tool: Net of Rectangular Prism* and *Math Tool: Net of Triangular Prism* to help you explore surface area and volume.

a. Measure the lengths of the dimensions of the nets using a ruler. Record the lengths.

b. Use those lengths to determine the total surface area and volume of the rectangular prism and the triangular prism. Record those measures in the table below.

	Surface Area	Volume
Rectangular Prism		
Triangular Prism		

c. Cut out each net and fold the nets to form prisms. Glue or tape the nets together.

d. The rectangular faces of both prisms have the same dimensions. Place the triangular prism on top of the rectangular prism so two congruent faces are resting on one another to form a composite solid.

e. What is the total surface area of the composite solid you just formed? Can you determine the total surface area by adding the surface areas you found above? Explain.

_____

_____

_____

f. What is the total volume of the composite solid you just formed? Can you determine the total volume by adding the volumes you found above? Explain.

_____

_____

_____

g. What can you conclude about finding the surface area and volume of a figure formed by putting two solid figures together?

_____

_____

_____

Grade 6 RP

Understand ratio concepts and use ratio reasoning to solve problems.

Grade 7 SP

Use random sampling to draw inferences about a population.

Draw informal comparative inferences about two populations.

Investigate chance processes and develop, use, and evaluate probability models.

Grade 8 SP

Investigate patterns of association in bivariate data.

Grade 6 SP

Develop understanding of statistical variability.

Summarize and describe distributions.

Domain 5
Statistics and Probability

25 Understanding Sampling

UNDERSTAND A **population** is a group of individuals or objects that you may want to study. If a population is too large for data to be collected from every member, you will need to collect data from a part, or a **sample**, of the population.

The best kind of sample to pick is a **random sample**. In a random sample, every member of a population has an equal chance of being selected. Because of this, random samples are often representative of the population as a whole. If the people or objects in a sample are representative of the larger population, then whatever inferences you make based on your sample will also be true about the population.

Be careful to avoid choosing a **biased sample**. A sample is biased if some members of a population are more likely to be chosen than others.

Consider this survey. Nina wants to know how the students in her school feel about the new dress code. She randomly selects the names of 100 students from a school list and e-mails each of them a survey. She waits for responses and records data from surveys that are returned to her. Is her sample biased?

1 Consider how Nina chose the students to whom she e-mailed the survey.
She randomly selected the names of students and e-mailed them the survey. So, her initial sample—the students she e-mailed the survey to—is likely to be a representative sample.

2 Consider the data she received and recorded.
Nina did not receive surveys back from every student she e-mailed. If she does not make additional efforts to gather information about those students, then her survey has what is known as voluntary response bias. The students who took the time to fill out and send back the survey are more likely to feel strongly about the school dress code. Students who may have less strong feelings may not have bothered to return the survey.

▶ Unless Nina attempts to collect data from those who did not respond to her survey, her sample will be biased because it will only include those who chose to respond to her e-mail.

Connect

Consider this survey. Tripp wants to know how the students in his school feel about the new dress code. He surveys all the students in his homeroom. Is his survey biased? If it is, what could he have done differently to make it representative?

1

Is Tripp's sample biased?

Yes, it is biased because not everyone in his school has a chance of being selected.

Only students in Tripp's homeroom can be selected. This means that students in other homerooms of his grade or in other grades will not be chosen.

This is an example of a convenience sample that was probably chosen because it was easy for Tripp to survey the students in his homeroom, since he sees them every day. Convenience samples are biased.

2

What could he have done differently?

The population he wants to study is all the students in his school. He could have found a way to randomly select students from that population.

For example, he could have surveyed every 10th student to arrive at school one day.

In that way, every student in his school would have an equal chance of being selected.

▶ Tripp's sample is biased because he only surveyed students in his homeroom. That is not representative of his entire school. He should have chosen a method that would let him randomly select students from his entire school for his sample.

DISCUSS

What if Tripp arrives at school early one morning? He surveys the first 50 students who arrive at school. Is this a good sample that is likely to be representative? Explain.

EXAMPLE A A researcher chose a random sample of registered voters in Kentsville. He found that 3 out of every 5 voters surveyed said they would vote for Miguel Miller for mayor. If there are 800 eligible voters in Kentsville, predict how many of those voters will choose Miguel Miller for mayor. Why would this be a valid inference to draw from these data?

1

Is the sample representative?

The sample was chosen randomly, so it is a representative sample.

2

Predict how many voters will vote for Miguel Miller in the general election.

If 3 out of 5 voters surveyed will choose Miguel Miller, then you can predict that $\frac{3}{5}$ of all 800 voters will choose Miguel Miller.

$$\frac{3}{5} \times \frac{800}{1} = \frac{2400}{5} = 480$$

▶ Since the sample is random, it is probably representative. A valid inference to draw would be that $\frac{3}{5}$ of the 800 voters in Kentsville, or about 480 voters, will vote for Miguel Miller in the general election.

TRY

Sarah randomly surveyed 80 students at her school. She found that 15 out of the 80 students she surveyed chose pizza as their favorite school lunch option. If there are 700 students at her school, predict how many students at her school would choose pizza as their favorite lunch option. If the answer you get is a decimal, how do you interpret that?

EXAMPLE B Anju wants to know the **mean** age, in months, of seventh-grade students at her school. She chooses 20 seventh-grade students at random to survey and records their ages, in months. Her data are below:

| 156 | 160 | 150 | 162 | 158 | 150 | 158 | 156 | 155 | 168 |
| 154 | 153 | 157 | 160 | 161 | 152 | 145 | 148 | 153 | 154 |

Estimate the mean age, in months, of a seventh-grade student at her school.

1

First, find the mean of the collected data.

$$\text{mean} = \frac{\text{sum of all numbers in set}}{\text{total number of numbers in set}}$$

The sum of all the ages is:

156 + 160 + 150 + 162 + 158 + 150 + 158 + 156 + 155 + 168 + 154 + 153 + 157 + 160 + 161 + 152 + 145 + 148 + 153 + 154 = 3,110

$$\text{mean} = \frac{3110}{20} = 155.5$$

2

Estimate the mean age of a seventh-grade student at Anju's school.

Since Anju chose a random sample, it is likely representative of all seventh-grade students at her school. So the mean age of her sample, 155.5 months, is a good estimate of the mean age of all seventh-grade students at her school. Since it is a decimal, round it up to the nearest whole number.

▶ A good estimate is 156 months.

CHECK

It is always useful to check that your answer is reasonable, especially when you must compute with many different numbers. Suppose Anju had computed 311 as the mean age. How could she know immediately that she had made an error?

Practice

Identify each sample as *random* or *not random*. Assume that the population to be studied is all students in a school.

1. Sam surveys every student in the school band.

   _____

2. Sam surveys every 8th student as the students arrive in the cafeteria.

   _____

Fill in each blank with an appropriate word or phrase.

3. A _____ is the group of people or objects that a researcher wants to study.

4. If a population is very large, a _____ of that population is selected and studied instead.

5. In a _____ sample, every member of a population has an equal chance of being selected.

6. In a _____ sample, some members of a population have a greater chance of being selected than others.

7. If a sample is representative of a population, data obtained from the sample can be used to make _____ about the larger population.

Khalid wants to find out if most students at his middle school would support using school money to buy new football equipment. Decide if each way of choosing a sample will result in a sample that is either representative or biased/flawed. If the sample is biased or flawed, explain why.

8. Khalid surveys every student attending a school football game.

   _____

9. Khalid surveys every 10th student entering the cafeteria during seventh-grade lunch.

   _____

10. Khalid selects the names of 50 students at random from a school directory and surveys them.

    _____

11. Khalid hands out surveys to 100 randomly chosen students, and he scores the surveys that are returned to him.

    _____

Solve.

12. Parents of students at a middle school were randomly selected to participate in a survey. Thirty-one out of 50 parents who were surveyed support extending the school day. There are a total of 420 parents with children at the middle school. Predict how many of those parents are likely to support extending the school day. Show your work.

_____

_____

13. Lindsey wants to find out, on average, how many hours per week seventh-grade students at her school spend studying. She decided to survey the students sitting in her social studies class to find out. Is her sample likely to be representative of all seventh-grade students at her school? Why or why not?

_____

_____

14. Oliver wants to know the mean number of pages in novels in his seventh-grade classroom. He randomly chooses 20 novels from his classroom library and records the total number of pages in each. His data are below.

| 180 | 150 | 200 | 212 | 232 | 300 | 290 | 175 | 210 | 234 |
| 240 | 199 | 160 | 150 | 178 | 290 | 212 | 205 | 205 | 170 |

Predict the mean number of pages in a novel in Oliver's classroom.

_____

_____

15. **PREDICT** Oliver asks his classmate Lilly to perform the same experiment he did. Lilly randomly chooses 20 novels from the classroom library and records the total number of pages in each. Her data are below.

| 212 | 199 | 220 | 160 | 278 | 200 | 290 | 175 | 300 | 180 |
| 200 | 150 | 200 | 154 | 152 | 210 | 224 | 205 | 215 | 160 |

Use Lilly's sample to predict the mean number of pages in a novel in Oliver's classroom. By how many pages does this prediction vary from Oliver's prediction? Explain why this variation is or is not reasonable.

_____

_____

Using Mean and Mean Absolute Deviation

UNDERSTAND The mean and **median** of a data set are used to measure where the center of a set of data lies. Other measures indicate how spread out, or how variable, data are. These measures include the **range**, the **interquartile range (IQR)**, and the **mean absolute deviation (MAD)**.

The MAD measures how much the data points in a set vary from the mean, $\bar{x}$. To find the distance of a data point from the mean, subtract the mean from the data point, x: $x - \bar{x}$. Since distances are always positive, you must take the absolute value of that difference to find the absolute deviation from the mean. The MAD is the mean of all the absolute deviations in the data set.

Calculate the MAD of this data set: 5, 8, 9, 11, 12.

1

Calculate the mean, $\bar{x}$.

$$\bar{x} = \frac{5 + 8 + 9 + 11 + 12}{5} = \frac{45}{5} = 9$$

2

Find the absolute deviation of each data point from the mean. Use a table to organize your work.

Data Point, x	Deviation from Mean, $x - \bar{x}$	Absolute Deviation from Mean, $\lvert x - \bar{x} \rvert$
5	$5 - 9 = -4$	$\lvert -4 \rvert = 4$
8	$8 - 9 = -1$	$\lvert -1 \rvert = 1$
9	$9 - 9 = 0$	$\lvert 0 \rvert = 0$
11	$11 - 9 = 2$	$\lvert 2 \rvert = 2$
12	$12 - 9 = 3$	$\lvert 3 \rvert = 3$

3

Calculate the mean of the absolute deviations.

$$MAD = \frac{4 + 1 + 0 + 2 + 3}{5} = \frac{10}{5} = 2$$

The mean absolute deviation is 2.

⊏ Connect

Rachel and Molly are in the same reading class. Rachel's scores on her first three vocabulary quizzes were 79, 86, and 90. Molly's scores were 70, 78, and 80. Calculate the means and the mean absolute deviations of their quiz scores. Compare them.

1

Calculate the MAD for Rachel's scores.

$$\bar{x} = \frac{79 + 86 + 90}{3} = \frac{255}{3} = 85$$

x	$x - \bar{x}$	$|x - \bar{x}|$
79	$79 - 85 = -6$	$|-6| = 6$
86	$86 - 85 = 1$	$|1| = 1$
90	$90 - 85 = 5$	$|5| = 5$

MAD for Rachel's scores $= \frac{6 + 1 + 5}{3}$

$$= \frac{12}{3} = 4$$

2

Calculate the MAD for Molly's scores.

$$\bar{x} = \frac{70 + 78 + 80}{3} = \frac{228}{3} = 76$$

x	$x - \bar{x}$	$|x - \bar{x}|$
70	$70 - 76 = -6$	$|-6| = 6$
78	$78 - 76 = 2$	$|2| = 2$
80	$80 - 76 = 4$	$|4| = 4$

MAD for Molly's scores $= \frac{6 + 2 + 4}{3}$

$$= \frac{12}{3} = 4$$

3

Compare the means and MADs.

Rachel and Molly have different mean scores, 85 and 76.

The difference in their mean quiz scores is: $85 - 76 = 9$ points.

The MAD for both sets of quiz scores is the same, 4 points.

▶ Rachel's mean quiz score is 9 points higher than Molly's. However, the variability in their quiz scores is essentially the same.

DISCUSS

What would be the result if you calculated the mean of the deviations from the mean $(x - \bar{x})$, instead of the mean of their absolute values, for the set of data above? Would the results tell you how variable the set of data is? Why or why not?

EXAMPLE A The table shows the number of books that a sample of students from two different reading classes read over the summer.

Class A	Class B
1, 3, 5, 7, 9	4, 5, 5, 5, 6

Calculate the mean and MAD of each. Compare those measures and make a dot plot for each set of data.

1

Find the mean and MAD for Class A.

$$\bar{x} = \frac{1 + 3 + 5 + 7 + 9}{5} = \frac{25}{5} = 5$$

x	x − x̄	|x − x̄|
1	1 − 5 = −4	|−4| = 4
3	3 − 5 = −2	|−2| = 2
5	5 − 5 = 0	|0| = 0
7	7 − 5 = 2	|2| = 2
9	9 − 5 = 4	|4| = 4

$$MAD = \frac{4 + 2 + 0 + 2 + 4}{5} = \frac{12}{5} = 2.4$$

2

Calculate the mean and MAD for Class B.

$$\bar{x} = \frac{4 + 5 + 5 + 5 + 6}{5} = \frac{25}{5} = 5$$

x	x − x̄	|x − x̄|
4	4 − 5 = −1	|−1| = 1
5	5 − 5 = 0	|0| = 0
5	5 − 5 = 0	|0| = 0
5	5 − 5 = 0	|0| = 0
6	6 − 5 = 1	|1| = 1

$$MAD = \frac{1 + 0 + 0 + 0 + 1}{5} = \frac{2}{5} = 0.4$$

3

Plot the data on dot plots. Compare the means and MADs.

Books Read
Class A

Class B

The center for both data sets is the same, but the Class A data is more spread out.

▶ The mean number of books read for both classes is the same, 5. However, the data for Class A is more variable.

DISCUSS

How many times greater is the MAD for Class A than for Class B? What does this show about the variability of the data sets? Explain.

EXAMPLE B The data below show the number of miles that randomly selected samples of members of two running clubs ran last week.

Club A	Club B
8, 10, 10, 14, 14, 20, 20, 24	10, 12, 12, 14, 14, 16, 18, 18

Create a double box-and-whisker plot for these data. Use it to make inferences about the running clubs from which the data are drawn.

1

Find the median, quartiles, and extremes for the Club A and Club B data sets.

The median of the Club A data set is 14: 8, 10, 10, <u>14</u>, <u>14</u>, 20, 20, 24

The median of the lower half of the data (lower quartile) is 10: 8, <u>10</u>, <u>10</u>, 14

The median of the upper half of the data (upper quartile) is 20: 14, <u>20</u>, <u>20</u>, 24

The extremes are 8 and 24.

The median of the Club B data set is 14: 10, 12, 12, <u>14</u>, <u>14</u>, 16, 18, 18

The lower quartile is 12: 10, <u>12</u>, <u>12</u>, 14

The upper quartile is 17 (the mean of 16 and 18): 14, <u>16</u>, <u>18</u>, 18

The extremes are 10 and 18.

2

Construct a double box-and-whisker plot. Use it to make inferences about the data.

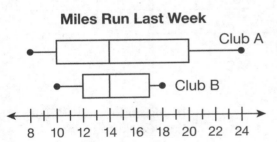

Miles Run Last Week

The samples were random, so they are probably representative of all members of the clubs. Both samples have the median 14. The data for the Club A sample is more variable because the box is wider and the whiskers extend farther to the left and to the right.

▶ On average, the number of miles run last week by members of both clubs was similar, about 14 miles per week. The data for Club B are less variable than the data for Club A, so the Club B members are probably more similar to one another in terms of experience level and how much they train each week. Club A likely has both beginners and more experienced runners.

DISCUSS

Calculate the range and interquartile range for the data in the box-and-whisker plot. Does this information support the inference that the runners in Club B are probably more similar in terms of time spent training than the Club A runners?

Practice

Calculate the mean of the data sets below.

1. Set M: $8.50, $8.50, $10.00

   Set N: $5.60, $7.40, $8.00

    HINT The mean is the sum of all the numbers in a set divided by the number of numbers in the set.

   mean of Set M = _____   mean of Set N = _____

Use the data below for questions 2–5.

Heights (in inches) of Starting Players, Girls' Basketball Team	Heights (in inches) of Starting Players, Boys' Basketball Team
64, 66, 66, 68, 71	67, 67, 69, 70, 72

2. Calculate the mean and MAD of the heights of starting players for the girls' team. Use the table. Show your work.

   $\bar{x}$ = _____

x	$x - \bar{x}$	$|x - \bar{x}|$
64		
66		
66		
68		
71		

   MAD = _____

3. Calculate the mean and MAD of the heights of starting players for the boys' team. Use the table. Show your work.

   $\bar{x}$ = _____

x	$x - \bar{x}$	$|x - \bar{x}|$
67		
67		
69		
70		
72		

   MAD = _____

4. On average, which team has taller starting players? Use the means you calculated above and the dot plots on the right.

   _____

5. On which team are the heights of the starting players more variable? Use the MADs you calculated above and the dot plots on the right.

   _____

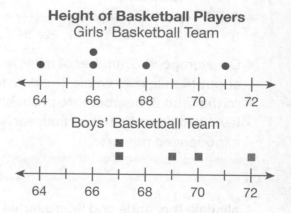

Height of Basketball Players
Girls' Basketball Team

Boys' Basketball Team

The box-and-whisker plot shows data collected from a randomly selected sample of competitive gymnasts who practice at two different gyms. It shows how many hours these gymnasts practice per week. Use the plot for questions 6 and 7.

6. On average, do competitive gymnasts from both gyms practice for about the same number of hours per week? Use the medians shown on the plot to support your answer.

_____

_____

Hours of Practice Per Week

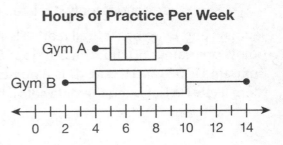

7. Based on these data, at which of these two gyms would you expect to have more gymnasts competing at different levels—some at lower levels, some in the middle, and some at higher levels? At which gym would you expect to have more gymnasts competing at similar levels? Use the range and IQR of the data, as well as the plot, to support your answer.

_____

_____

The dot plots show the ages of a random sample of students taken from a middle-school chorus and a sample of students taken from the all-school chorus in Lisa's hometown. Use these plots for questions 8–10. Show your work on a separate sheet of paper.

8. Calculate the mean age and MAD of members of the middle-school chorus.

mean = _____   MAD = _____

9. Calculate the mean age and MAD of members of the all-school chorus.

mean = _____   MAD = _____

10. CONCLUDE What conclusions can you draw about the average ages of chorus members, as well as the spread of the ages, in the two choruses? Use the measures you found above and the dot plots to support your answer.

Ages of Chorus Members
Middle School Chorus

All-School Chorus

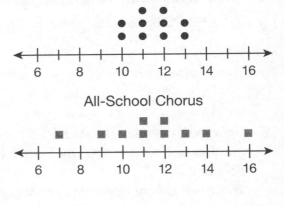

_____

_____

27 Making Comparative Inferences about Two Populations

UNDERSTAND The difference of the means divided by the quotient of the mean absolute deviations for two related data sets can tell how much the two sets overlap.

Teams A and B are basketball teams. In nine games, Team A scored the following numbers of points per game: 50, 53, 53, 55, 55, 55, 57, 57, and 60. The mean number of points scored per game is 55, and the MAD is 2 points. Team B has the same MAD. How much overlap will there likely be between the data sets if the mean for Team B is 65 points? 60 points? 55 points?

1

How much overlap is there if the mean number of points scored by Team B is 65 points?
In the plots, green squares represent data for Team A and blue circles represent data for Team B. There is very little overlap. Only one data point, 60, is shared by both sets.
The difference of the means divided by the MAD is: $\dfrac{65 - 55}{2} = \dfrac{10}{2} = 5$

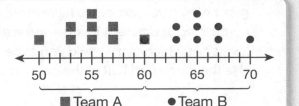

■ Team A   ● Team B

2

How much overlap is there if the mean number of points scored by Team B is 60 points?
As the plots show, there is partial overlap.
$\dfrac{\text{difference of means}}{\text{MAD}} = \dfrac{60 - 55}{2} = \dfrac{5}{2} = 2.5$

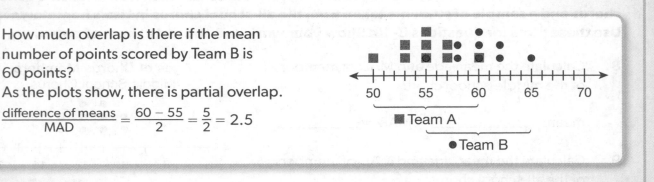

■ Team A
● Team B

3

How much overlap is there if the mean number of points scored by Team B is 55 points?
There will be complete or almost complete overlap. The plots show complete overlap.
$\dfrac{\text{difference of means}}{\text{MAD}} = \dfrac{55 - 55}{2} = \dfrac{0}{2} = 0$

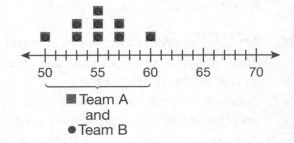

■ Team A
and
● Team B

▶ The plots above show how varying the mean from 65 to 60 to 55 can change the amount of overlap between the data sets for Teams A and B, which have the same variability.

⊏ Connect

The table shows the science test scores for two students in the same class. It also shows the mean and the mean absolute deviation for each set of test scores.

Claire	Richard
70, 75, 80, 80, 80, 80, 80, 80, 85, 90 mean = 80 MAD = 3	80, 88, 88, 90, 90, 90, 90, 92, 92, 100 mean = 90 MAD = 2.8

Use the difference of the means and the quotient of the MADs to predict how much the two data sets will overlap.

1

Find the difference of the means and the quotient of the MADs.

difference of means = 90 − 80
        = 10 points

quotient of MADs = 2.8 ÷ 3 ≈ 0.93

Since the quotient of the MADs is very close to 1, the data are similarly variable.

2

How much do you think the data will overlap?

The data are similarly variable and the difference of the means is 10 points.

The ratio of the difference of the means to the MAD is not 0, so the data will not overlap completely. However, since the MADs are close and the difference of the means is fairly small, I would expect the data sets to overlap partially.

3

Plot the data sets together to check your answer.

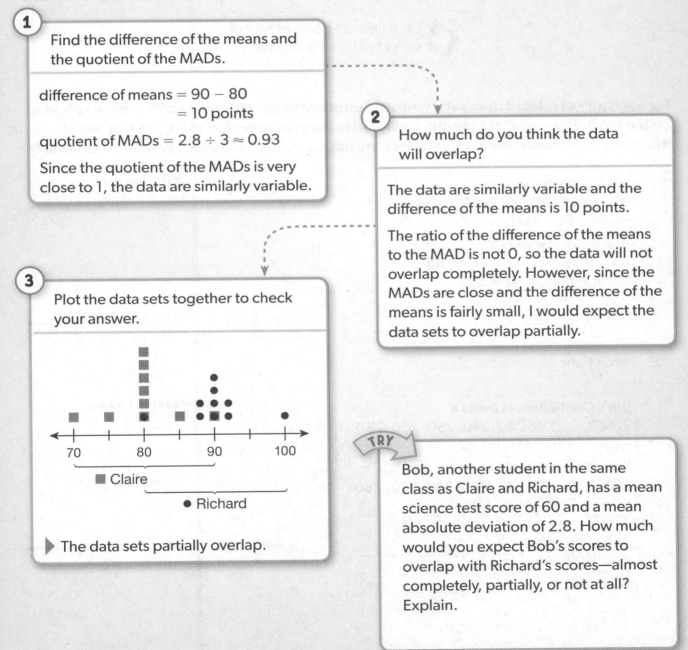

■ Claire

● Richard

▶ The data sets partially overlap.

TRY

Bob, another student in the same class as Claire and Richard, has a mean science test score of 60 and a mean absolute deviation of 2.8. How much would you expect Bob's scores to overlap with Richard's scores—almost completely, partially, or not at all? Explain.

Practice

Blue circles and green squares are used to indicate different sets of data on the dot plots below. Describe the overlap of the two data sets (*complete*, *partial*, or *none*).

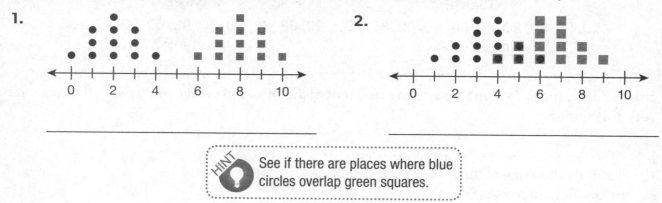

1.

2.

_____

_____

> **HINT** See if there are places where blue circles overlap green squares.

For each pair of related data sets, write the quotient of the difference of the means divided by the MAD. Then predict how much overlap (*almost complete*, *partial*, *little*, or *none*) there will be between the data sets. Plot the data on the grid to check your answer visually.

3.

Jane's Grades ●
80, 85, 90, 90, 90, 90, 95, 100
mean = 90   MAD = 3.75
Brandon's Grades ■
65, 70, 75, 75, 75, 75, 80, 85
mean = 75   MAD = 3.75

$\dfrac{\text{difference of means}}{\text{MAD}}$: _____

prediction: _____

Grades

65 70 75 80 85 90 95 100

4.

Jim's Cholesterol Levels ●
200, 230, 230, 240, 240, 250, 250, 280
mean = 240   MAD = 15
Yan's Cholesterol Levels ■
200, 220, 240, 240, 240, 240, 260, 280
mean = 240   MAD = 15

$\dfrac{\text{difference of means}}{\text{MAD}}$: _____

prediction: _____

Cholesterol Levels

180 200 220 240 260 280 300 320

5.

| Wages (Company A) ● |
| 8, 9, 10, 10, 10, 10, 11, 12 |
| mean = 10   MAD = 0.75 |

| Wages (Company B) ■ |
| 13, 14, 15, 15, 15, 15, 16, 17 |
| mean = 15   MAD = 0.75 |

$\dfrac{\text{difference of means}}{\text{MAD}}$: _____

prediction: _____

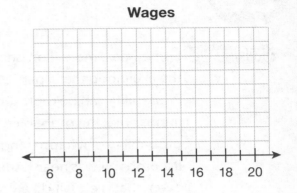

Wages

6   8   10   12   14   16   18   20

6. Below are measures for two samples.

Sample P: mean = 25, MAD = 5
Sample Q: mean = 30, MAD = 5

Which best describes how much the two data sets will overlap when graphed?

A. They will not overlap at all.

B. They will overlap a little.

C. They will overlap a lot.

D. They will overlap completely.

7. Below are measures for two samples.

Sample W: mean = 100, MAD = 5
Sample X: mean = 50, MAD = 5

Which best describes how much the two data sets will overlap when graphed?

A. They will not overlap at all.

B. They will overlap a little.

C. They will overlap a lot.

D. They will overlap completely.

Solve.

8. **PREDICT** On a separate sheet of paper, calculate the mean and MAD for each data set below. Use those values to predict how much the two data sets will, or will not, overlap. Then plot the data on the grid below at the right to check that your answer is correct.

| Ages of Volunteers (Hospital) ● |
| 14, 15, 15, 16, 16, 16, 16, 17, 17, 18 |
| Ages of Volunteers (Park) ■ |
| 17, 19, 20, 20, 20, 20, 20, 21, 21, 22 |

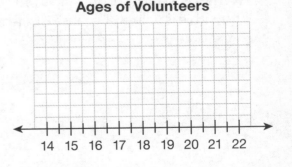

Ages of Volunteers

14   15   16   17   18   19   20   21   22

_____

_____

28 Understanding Probability

UNDERSTAND Sometimes, more than one outcome is possible for an event. If so, then the likelihood that a particular outcome will occur is called its **probability**. Probability can be represented as a number from 0 to 1. If an event is impossible, the probability of it happening is 0. If an event is certain, the probability of it happening is 1. If a probability is near 0, then it is unlikely. If a probability is near 1, then it is likely. A probability of $\frac{1}{2}$ refers to an event that is equally likely to occur or not occur. The ratio of the number of favorable outcomes to the number of possible outcomes is the **theoretical probability** of the event.

Julia has a bag with 15 colored marbles in it. The probability that Julia will draw a red marble from the bag is $\frac{1}{15}$. The probability that she will draw a green marble is $\frac{7}{15}$. Describe each of those outcomes using terms such as impossible, certain, likely, unlikely, or equally likely.

1

Is the probability of drawing a red marble, $\frac{1}{15}$, near 0, $\frac{1}{2}$, or 1?

```
      0.066...
15)1.000
   -90
    100
    -90
     10
```

The probability is 0.066…, which is close to 0.

▶ The probability of drawing a red marble is unlikely because it is near 0.

2

Is the probability of drawing a green marble, $\frac{7}{15}$, near 0, $\frac{1}{2}$, or 1?

```
      0.466...
15)7.000
   -60
    100
    -90
    100
    -90
     10
```

The probability is 0.466…, which is close to 0.5, or $\frac{1}{2}$.

▶ The probability of drawing a green marble is about equally likely to drawing a marble that is not green, because the probability is near $\frac{1}{2}$.

⊣⊏ Connect

You can conduct an experiment to help determine the probability of an event.

Theo spun a quarter on his desk and observed whether it landed heads up or tails up. He did this 50 times and recorded his results in the table.

Spinning a Quarter

	Number of Times
Heads	24
Tails	26
Total Trials	**50**

Determine the **experimental probability** of each outcome. Then use those experimental probabilities to predict the number of times you would expect the quarter to land heads up and tails up if you performed this experiment 80 times.

1

Find the experimental probability of the quarter landing heads up.

$$\text{experimental probability} = \frac{\text{number of times event occurs}}{\text{total number of trials}} = \frac{24}{50} = \frac{12}{25} = 0.48 = 48\%$$

2

Find the experimental probability of the quarter landing tails up.

$$\text{experimental probability} = \frac{\text{number of times event occurs}}{\text{total number of trials}} = \frac{26}{50} = \frac{14}{25} = 0.52 = 52\%$$

3

Predict the number of times you would expect the quarter to land heads up and tails up if you performed this experiment 80 times.

Multiply either the fractional probability or the decimal probability by 80.

Heads: $80 \cdot 0.48 = 38.4 \approx 38$ times   Tails: $80 \cdot 0.52 = 41.6 \approx 42$ times

▶ A good prediction would be that the quarter will land heads up 38 times and tails up 42 times. Since those numbers are so close, you could also predict that it would land heads up about $\frac{1}{2}$ the time (40 times) and tails up $\frac{1}{2}$ the time (40 times).

TRY

Cynthia drew a tile from a bag, recorded its color, and replaced it in the bag. The table shows her results.

If there are a total of 35 tiles in the bag, predict how many are silver.

Drawing Tiles

	Number of Times
Black	24
Silver	36
Total Trials	**60**

Practice

Identify each event as *impossible*, *likely*, *unlikely*, or *certain*.

1. The probability of tossing a number cube and getting 5 is $\frac{1}{6}$.

   _____

2. The probability of spinning blue on a spinner is 0.

   _____

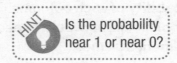

HINT   Is the probability near 1 or near 0?

Fill in the blanks.

3. _____ can be expressed as a number from 0 to 1 and is the likelihood that an event will occur.

4. The _____ of an event is the ratio of the number of times the event occurs in an experiment to the total number of trials.

5. If two outcomes are _____ likely, they have the same probability.

6. If an outcome is unlikely, it has a probability near _____.

7. If an outcome is likely, it has a probability near _____.

8. The _____ of an event is the ratio of the number of favorable outcomes to the number of possible outcomes.

Describe each event as *likely*, *unlikely*, or *neither likely nor unlikely*. Explain why.

9. The probability of selecting a red marble from a bag of marbles is 0.47.

   _____

   _____

10. The probability of selecting a tile with a vowel on it from a box of tiles is $\frac{3}{20}$.

    _____

    _____

11. The probability of a spinner landing on a shaded section is 53%.

    _____

    _____

12. The probability of tossing a number cube and rolling a number greater than 1 is $\frac{5}{6}$.

    _____

    _____

The table below on the right shows the results of choosing a tile from a bag with lettered tiles in it. Use the table for questions 13 and 14. Show your work for each question.

13. What is the experimental probability of randomly selecting the letter A from the bag? the letter B? Simplify answers if possible.

Drawing Tiles from Bag

	Number of Times
A	8
B	16
Total Trials	24

_____

_____

14. If there are a total of 9 tiles in the bag, predict how many of the tiles in the bag have the letter B on them.

_____

Solve. Assume that questions 15 and 16 involve the same spinner.

15. **PREDICT** The table shows the results of spinning a spinner 10 times. If you spin this spinner 40 times, predict how many times the spinner will land on a yellow section. Show your work and explain why your prediction may not be completely accurate.

Spinning a Spinner

	Number of Times
Blue	2
Orange	5
Yellow	3
Total Trials	10

16. **COMPARE** The table shows the results of spinning the same spinner 300 times. Compare the experimental probabilities for the two experiments. Which experimental probabilities give better estimates of the probability of spinning each color? Explain.

Spinning a Spinner

	Number of Times
Blue	75
Orange	150
Yellow	75
Total Trials	300

LESSON
29 Probabilities of Simple Events

UNDERSTAND You do not need to perform an experiment to identify a probability. If you have knowledge about an event and its outcomes, you can create a **probability model**. This model assigns a theoretical probability to each outcome, according to this ratio:

$$\text{theoretical probability} = \frac{\text{number of favorable outcomes}}{\text{number of possible outcomes}}$$

The favorable outcomes are the outcomes being considered. The set of all possible outcomes is called the **sample space**. The sum of the probabilities of all the outcomes is 1.

If each outcome in a chance process is equally likely, the probability model is called a **uniform probability model**.

Teresa flipped a fair coin 10 times. It landed heads up 6 times and tails up 4 times. What is the experimental probability of the coin landing heads up? What is the theoretical probability of the coin landing heads up? Are they the same or different? Explain.

1

Determine the experimental probability of the coin landing heads up.

$$\text{experimental probability} = \frac{\text{times event occurred}}{\text{total number of trials}} = \frac{6}{10} = \frac{3}{5}$$

2

Determine the theoretical probability of the coin landing heads up.
The sample space is: {heads, tails}. So, there are 2 possible outcomes.
There is 1 outcome being considered: heads. So, there is 1 favorable outcome.

$$\text{theoretical probability} = \frac{\text{number of favorable outcomes}}{\text{number of possible outcomes}} = \frac{1}{2}$$

3

Are the two probabilities the same or different?
The two probabilities are different, because the experimental probability indicates how many times the coin actually landed heads up, 3 out of every 5 tosses, while the theoretical probability shows how many times it was expected to land heads up, 1 out of every 2 tosses.

▶ The theoretical and experimental probabilities may or may not be the same. In this case, the theoretical probability of the coin landing heads up is $\frac{1}{2}$, but the experimental probability of that outcome was $\frac{3}{5}$.

⤎ Connect

There are 24 students in a class. If a student is selected at random from the class, what is the probability that Anna will be selected? What is the probability that Hector will be selected? What kind of probability model is being used in this situation?

1 Identify the probability of any one student being selected.

One student will be selected, so there is one favorable outcome.

There are 24 students in the class, so there are 24 possible outcomes.

$$\text{theoretical probability} = \frac{\text{number of favorable outcomes}}{\text{number of possible outcomes}}$$

$$\text{theoretical probability} = \frac{1}{24}$$

2 What is the probability, P, that Anna will be selected?

$$P(\text{Anna}) = \frac{1}{24}$$

$P(\text{Anna})$ is a way to represent the probability of selecting Anna.

3 What is the probability that Hector will be selected?

$$P(\text{Hector}) = \frac{1}{24}$$

4 What kind of probability model is being used?

▶ Since selecting any student from the class is equally likely, the probability model for this process is uniform. The probability of selecting any single student, including Anna or Hector, is $\frac{1}{24}$.

TRY

If it is equally likely that a girl will be selected as it is that a boy will be selected in this situation, what is the theoretical probability of selecting a girl? What is the theoretical probability of selecting a boy? Explain.

EXAMPLE A This spinner is divided into 8 equal-sized sections. What is the probability of the spinner landing on each of the colors shown? Why is the probability model for this spinner **not** an example of a uniform probability model?

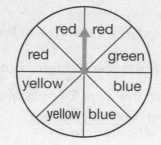

1

Identify the probability, P, of the spinner landing on each color.

There are 3 red sections. There are 8 sections in all.

$P(\text{red}) = \frac{3}{8}$

There is 1 green section, so:

$P(\text{green}) = \frac{1}{8}$

There are 2 blue sections, so:

$P(\text{blue}) = \frac{2}{8} = \frac{1}{4}$

There are 2 yellow sections, so:

$P(\text{yellow}) = \frac{2}{8} = \frac{1}{4}$

2

Explain why the probability model is not an example of a uniform probability model.

▶ A uniform probability assigns equal probability to each outcome. For this spinner, $P(\text{red}) = \frac{3}{8}$, $P(\text{green}) = \frac{1}{8}$, $P(\text{blue}) = \frac{1}{4}$, and $P(\text{yellow}) = \frac{1}{4}$, so the probabilities are not all equal.

TRY

If you were to spin the spinner shown above 120 times, how many times would you expect the spinner to land on red?

EXAMPLE B Two number cubes, each with faces numbered 1 to 6, are tossed at the same time. What is the probability of tossing a sum of 9?

1 Create a chart to show all the possible sums.

For example, the sum when a 1 is rolled on the first number cube and a 1 is rolled on the second number cube is: $1 + 1 = 2$.

First Number Cube

	1	2	3	4	5	6
1	2	3	4	5	6	7
2	3	4	5	6	7	8
3	4	5	6	7	8	9
4	5	6	7	8	9	10
5	6	7	8	9	10	11
6	7	8	9	10	11	12

Second Number Cube

The diagram shows that there are 4 ways to toss a sum of 9. So, there are 4 favorable outcomes.

2 What is the probability of tossing a sum of 9?

There are 36 possible outcomes in the chart. Four of them are favorable.

$P(\text{a sum of } 9) = \frac{4}{36} = \frac{1}{9}$

TRY

What is the probability of tossing the two number cubes and rolling a sum greater than 9? Explain.

Practice

Each spinner shown is divided into equal-sized sections. Identify the theoretical probability of each spinner landing on a shaded section, *P*(shaded). Simplify, if possible.

1.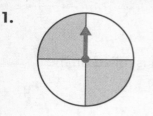

_____

2.

_____

3.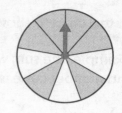

_____

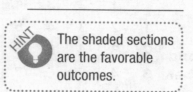

HINT — The shaded sections are the favorable outcomes.

Each bag contains lettered tiles, each the same size. Identify the theoretical probability of selecting the letter C from each bag. Simplify, if possible.

4. 5.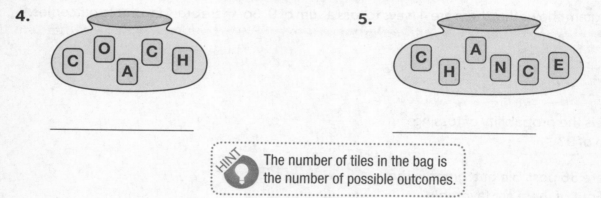

_____   _____

HINT — The number of tiles in the bag is the number of possible outcomes.

Choose the best answer.

6. The probability of reaching into a drawer without looking and selecting a black sock is $\frac{5}{6}$. If there are a total of 24 socks in the drawer, how many socks in the drawer are black?

A. 4

B. 6

C. 15

D. 20

7. There are 10 comedies and 15 dramas in a bargain bin of DVDs at a store. If Marcus reaches in and selects a DVD without looking, what is the probability that he will select a drama?

A. 0.15

B. 0.4

C. 0.6

D. 1.5

The spinner below on the right is divided into 5 equal-sized sections. Use the spinner for questions 8–10.

8. Write the sample space for this spinner.

_____

9. Identify P(even) and P(odd) for this spinner.

_____

10. If you spin the spinner 70 times, how many times would you expect the spinner to land on a section with a 2 on it? Show your work.

_____

Two number cubes, each with faces numbered 1 to 6, will be tossed at the same time. Use this situation for questions 11–13. Show or explain your work. Simplify, if possible.

11. What is the probability of tossing a sum of 7?

_____

12. What is the probability of tossing a sum greater than 7?

_____

13. What is the probability of tossing a sum less than 13?

_____

Solve. Simplify, if possible.

14. **EXPLAIN** Nadia tossed a number cube, with faces numbered 1 to 6, in the air 60 times. It came up 6 exactly 12 times. Determine the experimental probability and the theoretical probability of the cube coming up 6. Explain why it is reasonable that those two values are different.

_____

_____

_____

Probabilities of Compound Events

UNDERSTAND Sometimes, you may want to find the probability that two or more events will occur at the same time. This is called finding the probability of a **compound event**. Organized lists, diagrams, and tables can help you do this.

Imagine tossing two fair coins. The outcome of the first event does not affect the outcome of the second event. So, these are called **independent events**.

Imagine drawing a marble from a bag and, without replacing it, drawing a second marble from the bag. In this case, the outcome of the second event depends on the outcome of the first event. These are called **dependent events**.

For an experiment, Chad will toss a fair coin and a number cube with faces numbered 1 to 6 at the same time. What is the probability that the coin lands tails up and the cube comes up 2?

1

What are the possible outcomes for each event?
The possible outcomes for tossing a coin are: heads and tails.
The possible outcomes for tossing a number cube are: 1, 2, 3, 4, 5, and 6.
The outcome of tossing the coin does not affect the outcome of tossing the cube.
They are independent events.

2

Make a table to determine all the possible outcomes.

		Tossing Number Cube					
		1	**2**	**3**	**4**	**5**	**6**
Tossing Coin	**Heads**	H-1	H-2	H-3	H-4	H-5	H-6
	Tails	T-1	T-2	T-3	T-4	T-5	T-6

The table shows that there is one favorable outcome, T-2, out of 12 possible outcomes.

$$P = \frac{\text{number of favorable outcomes}}{\text{number of possible outcomes}} = \frac{1}{12}$$

▶ The probability of the coin landing tails up and the cube coming up 2 is $\frac{1}{12}$.

⊣€Connect

Each spinner below is divided into equal-sized sections. What is the probability that the first spinner will land on a shaded section and the second will land on the letter X?

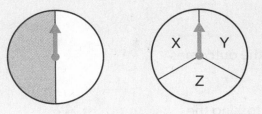

1 What are the possible outcomes for each spinner?

The possible outcomes for the first spinner are: shaded and unshaded.

The possible outcomes for the second spinner are: X, Y, and Z.

2 Make an organized list showing all the possible outcomes for spinning both spinners.

shaded-X	unshaded-X
shaded-Y	unshaded-Y
shaded-Z	unshaded-Z

3 What is the probability that the first spinner will land on a shaded section and the second will land on the letter X?

There is only 1 favorable outcome, shaded-X. There are 6 possible outcomes.

▶ The probability of the first spinner landing on a shaded section and the second landing on the letter X is $\frac{1}{6}$.

TRY

What would be the probability of the first spinner landing on a shaded section and the second spinner landing on the letter W? Explain.

EXAMPLE A Maya tosses a quarter and a dime into the air at the same time. Make a **tree diagram** to show all possible outcomes. Then determine the probability that both coins will land on tails.

1

Draw branches to show the outcomes of tossing the quarter.

The possible outcomes of tossing the quarter are heads (H) and tails (T).

Quarter

2

From the ends of the branches you already drew, draw additional branches to show the possible outcomes of tossing the dime.

The possible outcomes of tossing the dime are heads (H) and tails (T).

Draw 4 additional branches to show the outcomes of tossing the quarter and dime together.

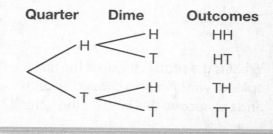

3

Determine the probability that both coins will land tails up.

There is 1 possible outcome in which both coins land tails up, TT.

There are a total of 4 possible outcomes.

▶ The tree diagram in step 2 shows the entire sample space. The probability of both coins landing tails up is $\frac{1}{4}$.

CHECK

Check your answer by using a different method to find all the possible outcomes and the probability of both coins landing tails up, such as making a table or an organized list. Show your work.

EXAMPLE B A bag contains 1 blue (B) and 2 green (G) marbles. Harrison will reach into the bag and pick a marble without looking. Without replacing the first marble, he will pick a second marble without looking. What is the probability that he will pick a green marble first and a blue marble second?

1 Use 3 branches to show the possible outcomes of Harrison's first pick.

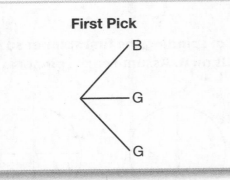

First Pick

B

G

G

2 Draw additional branches to show the possible outcomes of his second pick.

Since the first marble will not be replaced, the events are dependent.

If he picks a blue marble first, then he must pick a green marble second.

If he picks a green marble first, then he can pick either a blue marble or a green marble second.

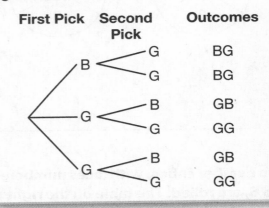

First Pick	Second Pick	Outcomes
B	G	BG
	G	BG
G	B	GB
	G	GG
G	B	GB
	G	GG

3 Determine the probability that he will pick a green marble first and a blue marble second.

There are 2 favorable outcomes, GB. There are 6 possible outcomes.

▶ The probability that Harrison will pick a green marble first and a blue marble second is $\frac{2}{6}$, or $\frac{1}{3}$.

DISCUSS

Suppose Harrison will replace the first marble before picking the second marble. How would that change the probability described above?

Practice

Identify each pair of events as *independent* or *dependent*.

1. drawing a marble from a bag, replacing it, and drawing a second marble

   _____

2. drawing a marble from a bag, not replacing it, and drawing a second marble

   _____

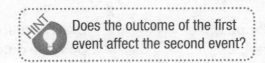

HINT   Does the outcome of the first event affect the second event?

For each pair of spinners, determine the probability of spinning the first spinner so it lands on 1 and spinning the second spinner so it lands on B. Assume each spinner is divided into equal-sized sections. Show your work.

3.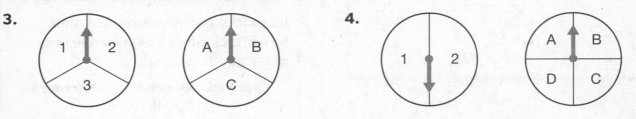

   _____

4.

   _____

Two number cubes, with faces numbered 1 to 6, are rolled. The table on the right can be used to represent all the possible outcomes of this experiment. Use the table for questions 5–7. Simplify if possible.

	1	2	3	4	5	6
1	(1, 1)					
2						
3						
4						
5						
6						

5. The outcome (1, 1) has been recorded for you in the table. This outcome shows rolling a 1 on each cube. Use ordered pairs to represent each outcome in the table.

6. What is the probability of rolling double 6s?

   _____

7. What is the probability of rolling doubles (two 1s, two 2s, etc.)?

   _____

In the tree diagram below on the right, R stands for a red tile and Y stands for a yellow tile. Use the tree diagram for questions 8 and 9.

8. The tree diagram represents the possible outcomes in an experiment in which Ben draws a tile from a bag without looking and records its color. He then draws a second tile from the bag and records its color. Based on the tree diagram, does Ben replace the tiles after the first draw, or not? Explain your reasoning.

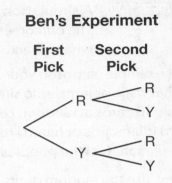

Ben's Experiment

First Pick   Second Pick

_____

_____

9. What is the probability that two tiles of the same color will be drawn in this experiment? Explain.

_____

_____

Solve.

10. **SHOW** Below is a number cube, with faces numbered 1 to 6, and a spinner divided into three congruent sections. Cassie will toss the cube and spin the spinner. What is the probability that her toss will result in a 2 and the spinner will land on a shaded section? Show your work.

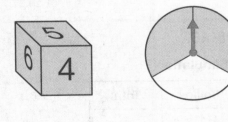

_____

11. **CREATE** The bag shown has 1 green (G) and 3 blue (B) marbles in it. Jayson will choose a marble from this bag, and without replacing it, he will choose a second marble from the bag. On a separate sheet of paper, create a tree diagram to show all the possible outcomes of this experiment. Then determine the probability that both marbles chosen will be blue.

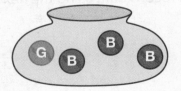

_____

31 Simulations

UNDERSTAND A **simulation** is a way of acting out a problem by conducting experiments. The outcomes of your simulation are comparable to, but not the same as, what the actual outcomes would be.

For example, suppose your neighbor recently started breeding dogs. Each puppy born will be either male or female. To simulate the first 10 puppies born, you can use a deck of 52 cards and draw 10 cards at random. Let each black card (spades or clubs) represent a male and each red card (diamonds or hearts) represent a female. You draw 6 black cards and 4 red cards. So, in this simulation, 6 of the puppies born are male and 4 are female.

Now, use the random digits in the table below to simulate the same event: the first 10 puppies born. Did you get the same result as above? Explain.

| 75922 | 89361 | 28145 | 27034 | 00280 |

1

Let odd digits represent male puppies and even digits represent female puppies. Start with any number in the table, such as 89361, and use tallies to represent each outcome.

8 is even, so draw a tally in the row for "females."
9 is odd, so draw a tally in the row for "males."
3 is odd, 6 is even, and 1 is odd. Draw tallies for those digits, too.

Puppy Simulation

	Tallies	Total
Male (odd)	|||	
Female (even)	||	

2

Now, record data using the next number in the table, 28145.

Puppy Simulation

	Tallies	Total
Male (odd)	⊬⊬	5
Female (even)	⊬⊬	5

1 and 5 are odd. ⟶ **Male (odd)**
2, 8, and 4 are even. ⟶ **Female (even)**

▶ The result is different. In this simulation, 5 puppies are male and 5 are female. It is reasonable that the two simulations had different results because a simulation produces only a possible result, not an actual result.

⟜€ Connect

Emma has a batting average of .300. Estimate the probability that she will get at least one hit in her next two times at bat by collecting data for 10 trials.

1

From Column A of *Math Tool: Random Digits Table*

Column A
91037
84668
56950
67392

Since the probability of Emma getting a hit is .300, we can use 3 digits from a random number table to represent hits. For example, the digits 0–2 can represent hits (H). All other digits can represent not getting a hit (N).

2

To simulate two times at bat, consider pairs of digits. Underline the digits 0, 1, and 2 when they appear, to indicate a hit.

The first two digits are 9<u>1</u>.
That represents NH.

The next two digits are <u>0</u>3.
That represents HN.

The next two digits are 78.
That represents NN.

3

Continue finding pairs of digits and determine what each represents.

The other pairs are: 46, 68, 56, 95, <u>0</u>6, 73, and 9<u>2</u>.

Those represent NN, NN, NN, NN, HN, NN, NH.

▶ $\frac{4}{10}$ of the trials resulted in at least one hit, so a good estimate of the probability that Emma will get at least one hit during her next two times at bat is $\frac{2}{5}$, or 40%.

TRY

Use *Math Tool: Random Digits Table*, starting at Column A, Row 1 and moving down. Perform a simulation, with 10 trials, to estimate the probability that Emma will get at least one hit on her next three times at bat. Show your work.

Practice

Use *Math Tool: Random Digits Table* for all simulations calling for the use of random digits.

For questions 1 and 2, start at Column A, Row 5, and move across the row. Complete the tally charts to simulate tossing a fair coin 10 times. What each digit represents is indicated below.

1. even digits represent heads (H)
odd digits represent tails (T)

	Tallies	**Total**
H (even)		
T (odd)		

2. digits 0–4 represent heads (H)
digits 5–9 represent tails (T)

	Tallies	**Total**
H (0–4)		
T (5–9)		

HINT The first set of digits you will use is 06807.

Describe one way to use the given object to perform the simulation described.

3. Use a deck of cards to simulate the answers given on a multiple-choice quiz, if each question has four answer choices—A, B, C, and D—and a student guessed every answer.

4. Use a number cube, with faces numbered 1 to 6, to simulate tossing two coins at the same time.

For question 5, start at Column E, Row 1, and move down the column. Use the random digits to fill in the chart. Then answer the question.

5. Simulate the birth orders of children for 20 families, each with two children. Let odd digits represent boys (B) and even digits represent girls (G). Estimate the probability that a family selected at random will have two boys.

	Tallies	**Total**
BB		
BG		
GB		
GG		

For question 6, start at Column A, Row 10, and move across the row. Use the random digits to perform a simulation. Show or explain your work.

6. Suppose 50% of the students in the school band are boys. Estimate the probability that a randomly selected group of 3 band members will include at least one boy. In your simulation, let odd digits represent boys and even digits represent girls. Perform 8 trials.

_____

_____

For question 7, use *Math Tools: Spinners*, a pencil, and a paper clip to perform a simulation.

7. Two out of every 7 seventh-grade students at Miava Middle School are in the chorus. Estimate the probability of randomly selecting 3 seventh-grade students and having at least one student be in the chorus. Perform 10 trials to determine your answer. Describe your simulation and your results.

_____

_____

For questions 8 and 9, start at Column C, Row 1, and move down the column. Use the random digits to perform 20 trials of each simulation.

8. SHOW Christina's batting average is .400. That means the probability of her getting a hit any time she is at bat is .400. Estimate the probability that it will take at least three times at bat for her to get a hit. Let the digits 0–3 represent hits and 4–9 represent not getting a hit. Perform 20 trials of a simulation to determine your answer. Show your work.

_____

_____

_____

9. PERFORM Trent successfully scores 90% of foul shots during basketball games. Estimate the probability that, if he is fouled and gets a second foul shot only if he makes the first foul shot, he will get to make a second foul shot. Let the digits 0–8 represent a successful first foul shot and the digit 9 represent a miss. Perform 20 trials of a simulation to determine your answer. Show your work.

_____

_____

_____

Describe each event as *likely*, *unlikely*, or *neither likely nor unlikely*.

1. randomly selecting a green (G) marble from this box

_____

2. spinning the letter B

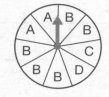

_____

Choose the best answer.

3. The box-and-whisker plot shows data collected from a randomly selected sample of test scores from two Spanish classes. Each class has the same teacher and took the same test on the same day. Which is a conclusion that can be drawn from these data?

Spanish Test Scores

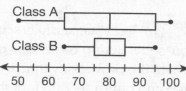

A. On average, students in Class A scored higher on the test than those in Class B.

B. On average, students in Class B scored higher on the test than those in Class A.

C. There was a greater range in the test scores for students in Class A than for those in Class B.

D. There was a greater range in the test scores for students in Class B than for those in Class A.

4. The table shows the results of an experiment in which Max drew tiles from a bag.

Drawing Tiles

	Number of Times
Red	9
Blue	46
Green	25
Total Trials	80

If Max conducts this experiment again and performs 200 trials, which is the best prediction of how many times he will draw a blue tile?

A. 58

B. 92

C. 100

D. 115

For each situation, determine the theoretical probability. Simplify, if possible.

5. There are 12 gumballs, each a different color, in a bag. One of them is red. What is the probability of reaching into the bag without looking and selecting a red gumball?

_____

6. There are 19 boys and 19 girls in the school pep band. If Trey randomly selects a member of the pep band to interview for the school newspaper, what is the probability that he will select a girl?

_____

Choose the best answer.

7. Below are measures for two samples.

   Sample S: mean = 20, MAD = 4
   Sample T: mean = 40, MAD = 4

   Which dot plot could represent data for the samples described above? (Assume that Sample S is represented by blue circles and Sample T is represented by green squares on the plot.)

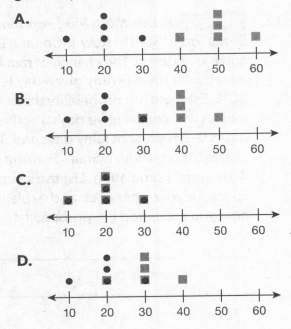

   A.

   B.

   C.

   D.

8. LaToya has a spinner that is divided into equal-sized sections, some shaded and some unshaded. She spun the spinner 100 times and recorded her results below.

   Spinning a Spinner

	Number of Times
Shaded	53
Unshaded	47
Total Trials	100

   Which are the best estimates of the theoretical probabilities of spinning each outcome on the spinner?

   A. shaded: $\frac{1}{2}$, unshaded: $\frac{1}{2}$

   B. shaded: $\frac{1}{3}$, unshaded: $\frac{2}{3}$

   C. shaded: $\frac{1}{4}$, unshaded: $\frac{3}{4}$

   D. shaded: $\frac{5}{11}$, unshaded: $\frac{6}{11}$

Choose the best answer.

9. Andre wants to find out which candidate for school president most students at his middle school will choose on election day. Surveying which of the following groups would produce the most representative sample?

    A. members of last year's student council

    B. every student in his English class

    C. the first 50 students who arrive at school one day

    D. 50 students whose names are selected randomly from the school directory

For question 10, assume that the sample is representative.

10. A survey found that 3 out of every 8 voters in Tallytown support a new law that prohibits people from walking their dogs in town parks. If there are 4,800 voters in Tallytown, estimate the number of voters who support the new law.

_____

Solve.

11. **CREATE** Below are two bags, each filled with same-sized lettered tiles. Pablo will reach into each bag and draw a tile without looking. Create a sample space to show all the possible outcomes of his experiment. Then determine the probability that Pablo will choose two tiles with the same letter on them. Explain how you found your answer.

_____

_____

12. **WRITE MATH** Use *Math Tool: Random Digits Table*. Start at Row 1, Column D, and move down. The chance of rain for a particular town on any given day is 30%. Estimate the probability that it will rain on two consecutive days. Let the digits 0–2 represent rainy days and 3–9 represent days with no rain. Perform 40 trials of a simulation. List the sample space for your simulation and explain how you estimated the probability.

_____

_____

_____

Paper Cup Toss

Working in pairs or individually, you will take a paper cup and toss it so that it spins in the air. If you do this, it will land in one of three ways: right side up, upside down, or on its side.

a. Before you begin, make a prediction about how many times you think the cup will land each way. Do you think each outcome is equally likely? If not, which outcomes do you predict will be more likely or less likely?

right side up   upside down   on its side

_____

b. Perform 30 trials of the experiment. Record each result in the "Tallies" column of the chart below. When you are finished, add up the tallies and fill in the "Frequency" column.

Group Results

	Tallies	Frequency	Experimental Probability
Right Side Up			
Upside Down			
On Its Side			

c. You can use data from an experiment to develop a probability model. First, determine the experimental probability of each outcome based on your results. Record those probabilities in the chart above. How close do you think those experimental probabilities are to the theoretical probabilities? Explain.

_____

d. The more trials you perform, the closer the experimental probability will get to the theoretical probability. Instead of performing additional trials, speak with your classmates and add their data to your data. Then fill in the chart below.

Class Results

	Frequency	Experimental Probability
Right Side Up		
Upside Down		
On Its Side		

e. Using the Class Results chart, estimate the theoretical probability of each outcome. Explain how you determined your estimates. (There is no one correct answer.)

_____

f. Did your final results match the prediction you made before you began the experiment? Explain.

_____

Glossary

additive inverses addends whose sum is 0 (Lesson 5)

adjacent angles non-overlapping angles that share a common side and a common vertex (Lesson 22)

area the number of square units inside a figure (Lesson 21)

associative property a property of addition and multiplication that states that the order of the groupings of numbers will not affect the answer (Lessons 6, 7)

biased sample a sample in which some members of the population have a greater chance of being selected for the sample than other members (Lesson 25)

circumference the distance around a circle (Lesson 21)

coefficient the number that is multiplied by a variable, such as 2 in 2x (Lesson 12)

commutative property a property of addition and multiplication that states that the order of the two addends or factors does not affect the sum or product (Lessons 6, 7)

complementary angles two angles whose measures have a sum of 90° (Lesson 22)

complex fraction a fraction in which the numerator and/or denominator is a fraction or a mixed number (Lesson 1)

compound event a combination of two or more events in a probability experiment (Lesson 30)

cone a three-dimensional figure with one circular base and one point called the apex or vertex (Lesson 20)

constant of proportionality the constant ratio by which two quantities co-vary in a proportion; also called the unit rate or constant ratio (Lesson 2)

cross section a two-dimensional view sliced by a plane through a three-dimensional figure (Lesson 20)

cylinder a three-dimensional figure with two congruent, parallel bases that are circles (Lesson 20)

dependent (event) an event in which the first outcome affects the second outcome (Lesson 30)

distributive property a property of multiplication that states that the product of a number multiplied by the sum of two addends is the same as the sum of the product of the number and each addend (Lesson 7)

experimental probability the ratio of the total number of times that the favorable outcome occurs to the total number of trials in a probability experiment (Lesson 28)

factoring dividing all the terms of an expression by their greatest common factor (Lesson 13)

greatest common factor (GCF) the largest number common to two or more terms (Lesson 13)

independent (event) an event in which the first outcome does not affect the second outcome (Lesson 30)

inequality a mathematical sentence that compares two unequal expressions (Lesson 17)

integers the set of positive whole numbers, their opposites, and zero (Lesson 5)

interquartile range (IQR) the difference between the third (upper) and first (lower) quartiles in a data set (Lesson 26)

like terms terms that have no variable or terms that have the same variable raised to the same power (Lesson 12)

mean the sum of the terms in a data set divided by the number of terms in the set (Lesson 25)

mean absolute deviation (MAD) the average of the absolute deviations from the mean (Lesson 26)

median the middle term, or the mean of the two middle terms, in a data set that is numerically ordered (Lesson 26)

multiplicative inverses factors whose product is 1 (Lesson 7)

origin the point named by (0, 0) on a coordinate grid, where the axes intersect (Lesson 2)

population the group of interest in a survey (Lesson 25)

prism a three-dimensional figure having two congruent, parallel bases that are polygons and having rectangular faces (Lesson 20)

probability the likelihood of a particular outcome for a chance event (Lesson 28)

probability model a way of assigning probabilities to a chance process by examining the process (Lesson 29)

proportion an equation that shows that two ratios are equivalent (Lesson 2)

pyramid a three-dimensional figure having one base that is a polygon and having triangular faces (Lesson 20)

radius the distance from the center of a circle to any point on the circle (Lesson 21)

random sample a sample in which each individual in the population has an equal chance of being selected for the sample (Lesson 25)

range the difference between the greatest value and the least value in a data set (Lesson 26)

rate a ratio that compares two quantities that have different units of measure (Lesson 1)

ratio a comparison of two numbers, written as $\frac{a}{b}$, $a{:}b$, or a to b (Lesson 1)

rational number a number that can be expressed as the ratio $\frac{a}{b}$ where a and b are integers and $b \neq 0$ (Lesson 5)

reciprocal a fraction that reverses the denominator and numerator of another fraction; also called a multiplicative inverse (Lesson 8)

sample a smaller group taken from a population (Lesson 25)

sample space the set of all possible outcomes for a probability experiment (Lesson 29)

scale the part of a scale drawing that tells how much the actual object has been reduced or enlarged (Lesson 18)

scale drawing a representation of an object that is proportional to the actual object (Lesson 18)

simulation a way of acting out a problem by conducting an experiment similar to the problem that needs to be solved (Lesson 31)

solid figure a figure that has length, width, and height; also called a three-dimensional figure (Lesson 20)

solution set the solutions of an inequality (Lesson 17)

sphere a three-dimensional figure in which every point on its surface is equidistant from its center (Lesson 20)

supplementary angles two angles whose measures have a sum of 180° (Lesson 22)

term a part of an algebraic expression (Lesson 12)

theoretical probability the ratio of the number of ways an event can occur (favorable outcomes) to the total number of possible outcomes (Lesson 28)

three-dimensional figure a figure that has length, width, and height; also called a solid figure (Lesson 20)

tree diagram a representation that uses branches to show all the possible outcomes for a probability experiment (Lesson 30)

uniform probability model a probability model in which equal probability is assigned to all outcomes (Lesson 29)

unit rate a rate in which the second quantity in the comparison is 1 unit (Lesson 1)

variable a letter or symbol that represents an unknown value (Lesson 12)

vertical angles two non-adjacent angles formed by intersecting lines; vertical angles are congruent (Lesson 22)

Math Tool: Rational Numbers Game

Operations Spinner

Number Type Spinner

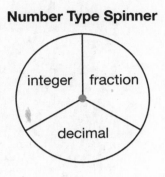

Integer Strips

0	1	2	3	4
–1	–2	–3	–4	–5

Fraction Strips

$\frac{1}{2}$	$\frac{1}{3}$	$\frac{1}{4}$	$\frac{2}{3}$	$\frac{3}{4}$
$\frac{1}{12}$	$\frac{1}{8}$	$\frac{1}{10}$	$\frac{1}{5}$	$\frac{2}{5}$

Decimal Strips

0.1	0.2	0.3	0.4	0.5
0.01	0.05	1.5	2.5	3.5

Chart

	Addition +	Subtraction –	Multiplication ×	Division ÷
Integers				
Fractions				
Decimals				

Math Tool: Number Properties and Rules

Addition Properties
Associative Property of Addition $(a + b) + c = a + (b + c)$
Commutative Property of Addition $a + b = b + a$
Additive Identity Property of 0 $a + 0 = a$
Sum of Additive Inverses $a + (-a) = 0$

Multiplication Properties
Associative Property of Multiplication $(a \times b) \times c = a \times (b \times c)$
Commutative Property of Multiplication $a \times b = b \times a$
Multiplicative Identity Property of 1 $a \times 1 = a$
Product of Multiplicative Inverses $a \times \frac{1}{a} = 1$

Addition and Multiplication
Distributive Property of Multiplication over Addition $a \times (b + c) = (a \times b) + (a \times c)$
Distributive Property of Multiplication over Subtraction $a \times (b - c) = (a \times b) - (a \times c)$

Properties of Equality	
Addition Property of Equality If $a = b$, then $a + c = b + c$.	Multiplication Property of Equality If $a = b$, then $a \times c = b \times c$.
Subtraction Property of Equality If $a = b$, then $a - c = b - c$.	Division Property of Equality If $a = b$ and $c \neq 0$, then $a \div c = b \div c$.

Math Tool: Area Formulas (Polygons)

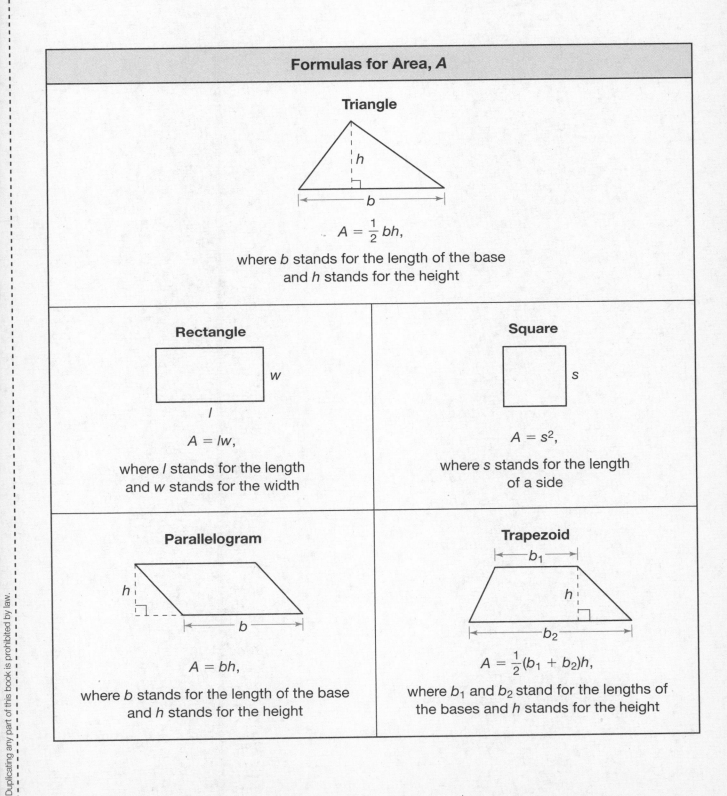

Formulas for Area, A

Triangle

$A = \frac{1}{2}bh,$

where b stands for the length of the base
and h stands for the height

Rectangle

$A = lw,$

where l stands for the length
and w stands for the width

Square

$A = s^2,$

where s stands for the length
of a side

Parallelogram

$A = bh,$

where b stands for the length of the base
and h stands for the height

Trapezoid

$A = \frac{1}{2}(b_1 + b_2)h,$

where b_1 and b_2 stand for the lengths of
the bases and h stands for the height

Math Tool: Circumference and Area Formulas (Circles)

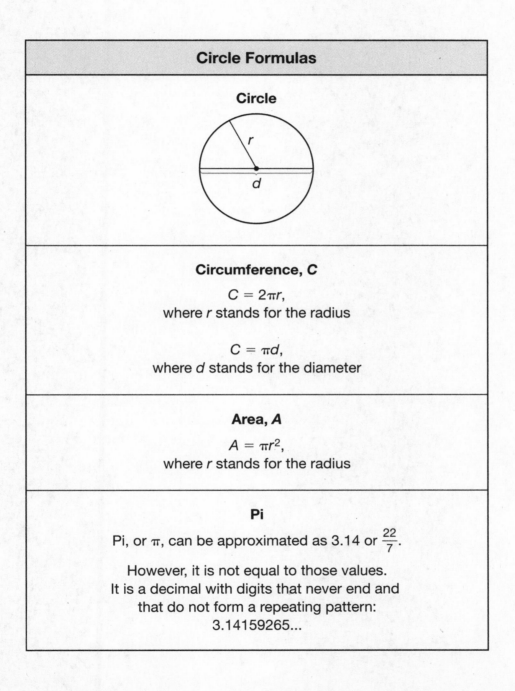

Circle Formulas

Circle

Circumference, C

$C = 2\pi r$,
where r stands for the radius

$C = \pi d$,
where d stands for the diameter

Area, A

$A = \pi r^2$,
where r stands for the radius

Pi

Pi, or π, can be approximated as 3.14 or $\frac{22}{7}$.

However, it is not equal to those values.
It is a decimal with digits that never end and
that do not form a repeating pattern:
3.14159265...

Math Tool: Volume Formulas

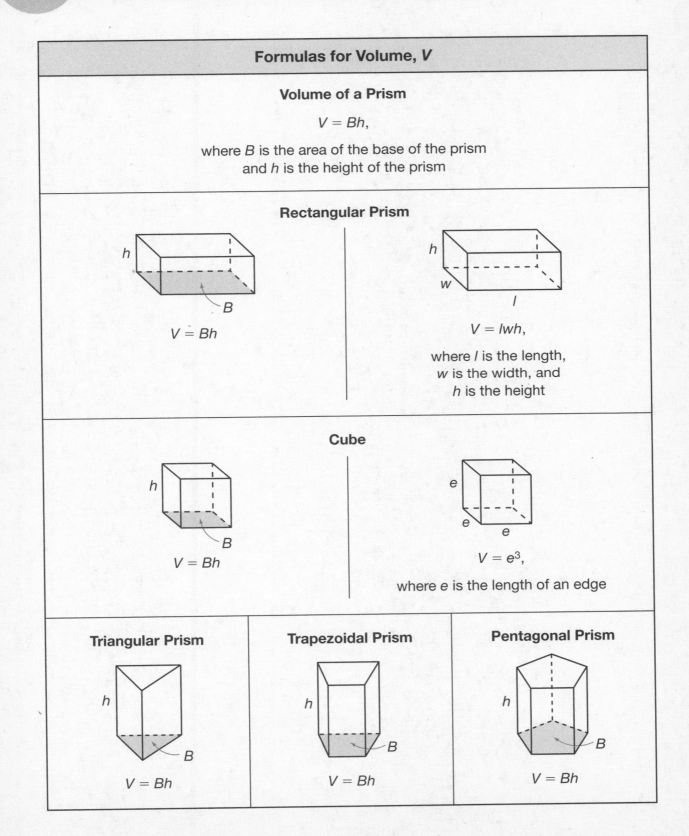

Formulas for Volume, V

Volume of a Prism

$V = Bh,$

where B is the area of the base of the prism
and h is the height of the prism

Rectangular Prism

$V = Bh$

$V = lwh,$

where l is the length,
w is the width, and
h is the height

Cube

$V = Bh$

$V = e^3,$

where e is the length of an edge

Triangular Prism

$V = Bh$

Trapezoidal Prism

$V = Bh$

Pentagonal Prism

$V = Bh$

Math Tool: Net of Rectangular Prism

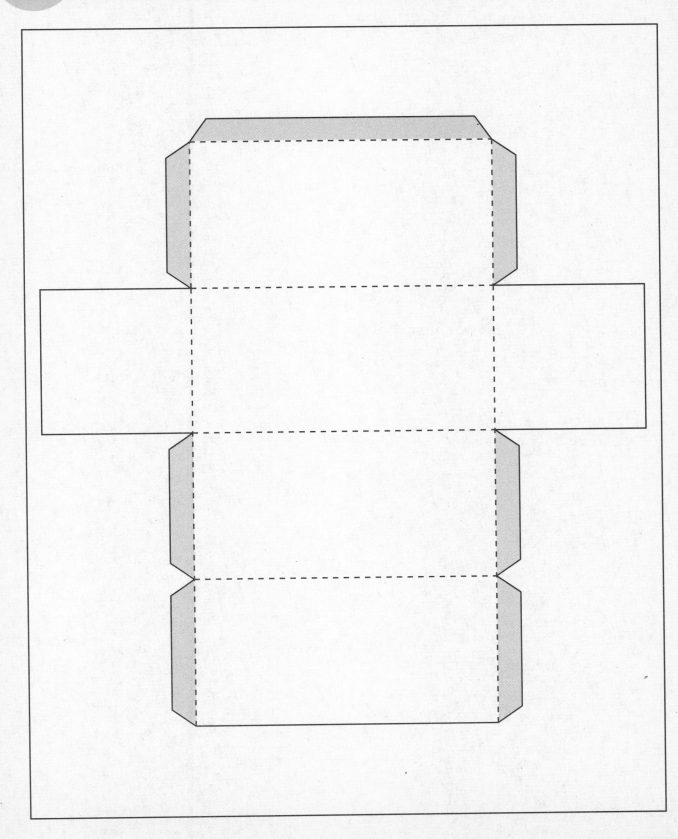

Math Tool: Net of Triangular Prism

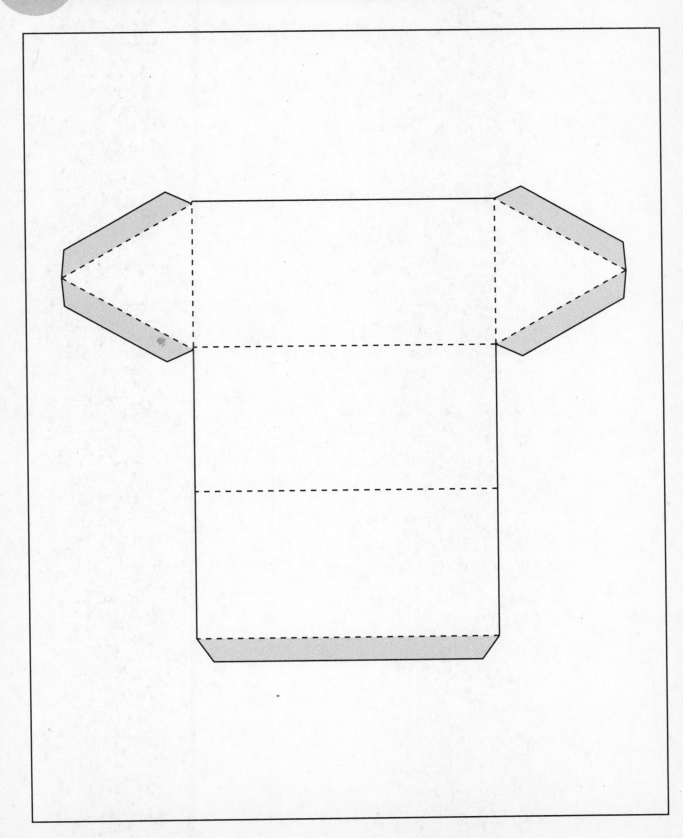

Math Tool: Number Lines on Grids

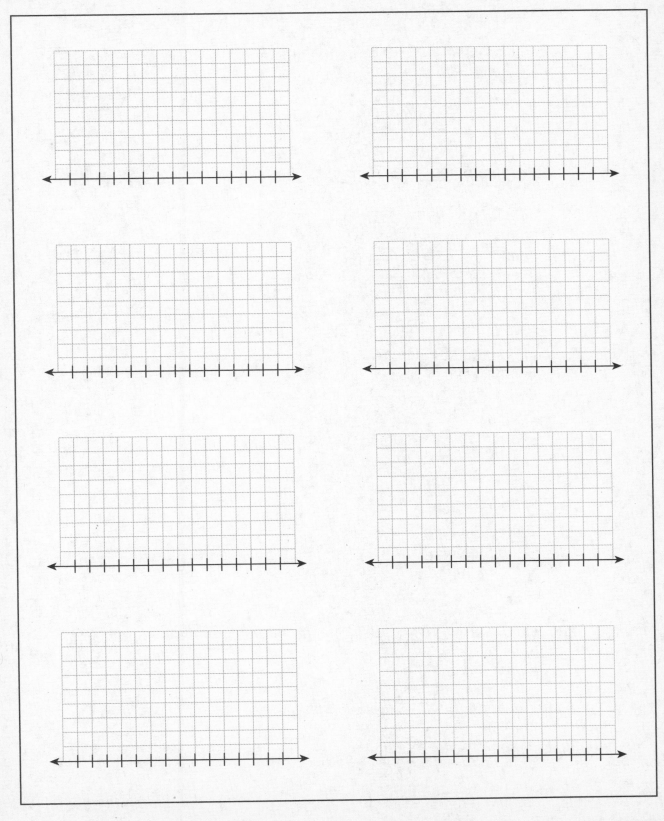

Math Tool: Random Digits Table

	Column A	Column B	Column C	Column D	Column E
Row 1	91037	01830	73685	14234	95784
Row 2	84668	77637	41367	23475	34210
Row 3	56950	64445	28573	08664	29604
Row 4	67392	97474	65078	59275	93318
Row 5	06807	77506	39982	67637	68692
Row 6	29604	86954	53998	20199	31988
Row 7	65078	42224	75730	69243	30378
Row 8	41855	97315	63915	27583	65907
Row 9	03289	30523	48623	94711	24911
Row 10	65228	81507	27341	37878	77825
Row 11	83015	06319	17822	96544	56959
Row 12	91119	33927	52551	85700	01759
Row 13	22360	86438	46415	89716	63517
Row 14	82415	62248	88109	53840	32896
Row 15	69853	57770	21895	31339	17840
Row 16	43071	04293	28209	12917	57452
Row 17	28723	91258	50682	78228	33640
Row 18	36734	55627	71635	36368	14382
Row 19	37878	69390	16093	43120	33900
Row 20	73360	09614	59553	23694	06646
Row 21	14577	42997	66483	39475	98730
Row 22	35124	26576	07627	50604	32544
Row 23	76413	90615	71272	24304	08904
Row 24	31649	48910	27354	84734	05383
Row 25	99054	32704	64569	57109	78553

Math Tool: Spinners

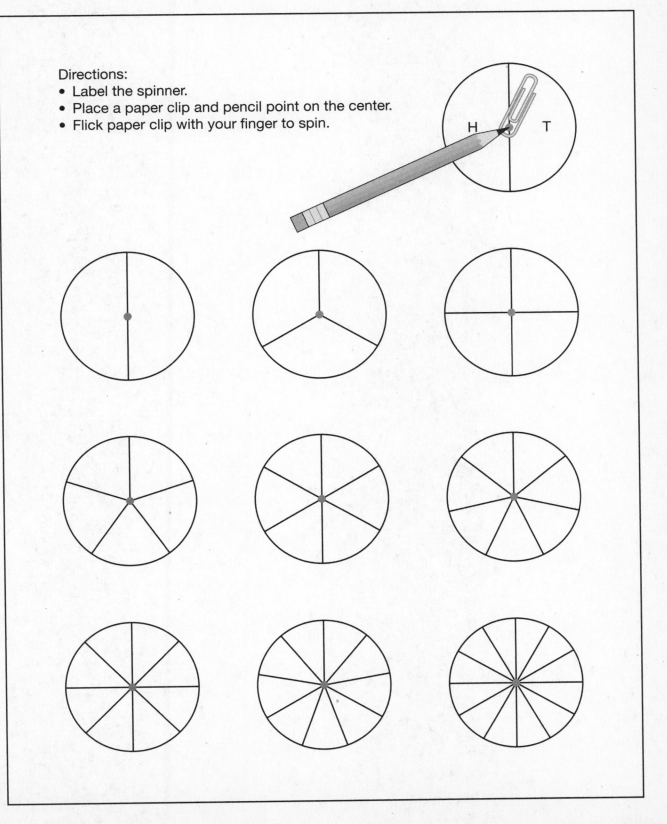

Directions:
- Label the spinner.
- Place a paper clip and pencil point on the center.
- Flick paper clip with your finger to spin.

H   T